Ladies and Gentlemen!

Daring to Live What the Soul Already Knows

Ladies and Gentlemen!

Daring to Live What the Soul Already Knows

*To Neal
whose service to others
extends the positive in
their lives —
John*

Demonstrating Fun, Ease, Joy, And the Healing Power of Common Sense

John J. Heney

John Heney

Published by

 GENERAL STORE
PUBLISHING HOUSE

Box 28, 1694B Burnstown, Ontario, Canada K0J 1G0
Telephone (613) 432-7697 or 1-800-465-6072

ISBN 1-894263-81-2

Printed and bound in Canada

Editing: Jane Karchmar
Cover Design: Brook Dunning
Layout: Derek McEwen
Portrait Photo: Moffitt, Sernoski & Jones

©John J. Heney

No part of this book may be reproduced, stored in a retrieval system or transmitted in any form or by any means, without the prior written permission of the publisher or, in case of photocopying or other reprographic copying, a licence from ACCESS COPYRIGHT (Canadian Copyright Licensing Agency), 1 Yonge Street, Suite 1900, Toronto, Ontario, M5E 1E5.

National Library of Canada Cataloguing in Publication

Heney, John J., 1956-
    Ladies and gentlemen! : daring to live what the soul already knows / John J. Heney.

ISBN 1-894263-81-2

    1. Common sense—Psychological aspects. 2. Success. 3. Self-help techniques. I. Title.

BF637.S8H35 2003   158.1   C2003-902501-2

*Dedicated to the
spirituality and sense of service
demonstrated by Dianne Stine Thomas (1949–2000),
publisher, seeker, friend and confidant.*

*Her desire to connect, to make connections,
to share friends
and to apply communication for the good of all
is still producing results!*

(Yahoo!)

Also by John Heney:

The Thunder Within

Contents

Forward!   11

A. My Card . . .   13
Getting to know me.

B. Coming to Terms with Spirituality and Stepping Up to Bat   17
Thought, intent, religion, prayer, concentration—whatever you call it—is energy. It has an effect and creates a reaction. It's a sea of interaction we are all living in, and that's where the fun begins.

C. When Talking It Becomes Living It   25
Adventures in group interaction: how people really are daring to share insights, deep truths and approaches that make sense.

D. A Treasury of Case Histories and Other Observations   31

    1 Walking around the Hurdles   31
    Setting aside obstacles that others gave you or that were not there in the first place.

    2 Stop Stopping Doing This!   34
    Be the first kid on the block to stop beating yourself over the head. Then you'll have a chance to look around.

    3 Listen Up!   38
    The power of the declaration. Owning up to the fact that we are all connected is no weird phenomenon. What you say is heard. Energy follows intent.

    4 Being There   42
    Getting over, under, through, around and past fear.

    5 Ironing Things Out   45
    As long as what you put out comes back, put out with creativity.

    6 Childhood Issues in Iceland (and Other Obstacles)   48
    Laugh at what we do to ourselves and be kind to ourselves, too.

7 Serving Where You Are   52
Making a difference exactly where you are can be fun, fascinating and inspiring.

8 One Doggone Ghost Story   56
Be prepared to move the entire environment to a completely new place where there is play and growth.

9 A Friend Comes Calling   59
Take the time to bring refreshing energy into people's homes and places of work and worship. Play with energy, by example.

10 A Busman's Holiday   64
Doing produces the change, and the change produces opportunity and confirmation.

11 How We Heal; How We Choose to Heal   70
Our reactions have a way of becoming far too complicated. Set an example: Use some common sense.

12 Sharing the Wealth   72
Knowing you are participating in an influence much bigger than yourself, and knowing that your presence counts, results in living what the soul knows.

13 Play Ball!   76
Dare to imagine. Walk through the marketplace with an energy that glows, and let your presence do the teaching.

14 Stretch the Table!   79
If you want joyous encounters, bring them with you.

15 Living Like It's Never Too Late . . . And Getting There Early   82
Because life goes on—and on—use your circumstance to inspire those around you and those who may later face your challenge. Demonstrate to others that growth is growth and to achieve it where it is least expected is a marvellous thing!

Contents

16 The Visit — 86
Be prepared to listen. What you put out can attract like-minded souls whose presence can strengthen our lives in helping each other. Events some believe to be unusual can be more common than we think.

17 Lost in the Woods — 90
Be prepared to embrace the realities of others. It is not that mystical things happen, it is often that we give them no place in our lives.

18 The 20–80/60–40/90–10 Rule — 93
When you're going through change, perhaps illness, stop and check. It might not be something you have to deal with—it might not be your problem.

19 The Nurse — 97
Bring what you desire, rather than hoping you'll find it. Know that there is more in common among us than meets the eye, and acknowledge this.

20 It's All Been Done Before (Again) — 100
Some of our dramas are ages old; our attitudes about them can become new.

21 The Eyes Have It! — 103
When you speak to energy, declare how your intent also helps others.

22 An Afterthunk — 108
How to approach healing work so that it uplifts, enhances, and supports people on behalf of themselves and all others who require healing.

23 The Art of the Spiritual High-Five — 111
Being in compassion saves time and effort. Helping each other along in gratitude inspires a refreshing way to make progress. If always the healer, you may need permission; but forever the demonstrator, the gates open wide.

24 The Pub — 113
If you are seeking an atmosphere, be bold enough to bring it. Show how it arrives and it will be there.

25 Gotcha!   **117**
Let the image do the talking.

26 You Go First!   **121**
Experience the thrill of daring to make things easier as you show the way.

E. Some Thoughts on What the Soul Already Knows   **125**

F. Daring to Live What the Soul Already Knows   **133**

About the Author   **137**

Forward!

Side effects from reading this book and using its principles may include relief, laughter, and the occasional bursting of declarations of "Oh [read *Poop*]!" (One day a lawyer called me to report how he had uttered exactly that [well, not exactly *that*] while he was reading my first book. Fortunately for all concerned he was actually perched on the toilet at the time. Funny things happen to you when you're a writer—you hear all kinds of stories about when, why and how people read your material. No connection is to be made between the phenomena of lawyers and toilets here. That's another book altogether about thought and energy!)

Whenever you next turn a corner, you encounter yet another of life's little dramas. We are magical little drama makers. It's nothing less than astonishing what we create in our heads and what boxes we put around our realities!

This being more or less a cosmic truth, I hope this book supplies you—in a respectful, energizing and gentle way—with examples of how we interpret life, so you too can laugh at what we create, so you can play *more* and move your strategies from that of fixing things to one that causes people to blossom. I want this book to help you become passionate about fun, ease, and joy; and to become strong enough to move among your neighbours and create new and *uplifting* stories. My eternal thanks to you and others who chose to show me through the stories of your own journey how all of this "life" stuff works. Such is the calling of a man who brings to others whatever it takes to help a person become joyous and satisfied. It's the work of one who plays and who studies thought and energy. The spiritual mechanic. The treasure hunter.

My credentials can be found in the pages of *The Thunder Within*, first published in 1999 under the encouragement of Dianne Stine

Thomas. Her sudden and untimely passing in a single-vehicle accident a year later pushed things forward for *so* many people around her, not the least of whom were those who would gather with her in discussion and exploration to bring new light on how available, easy, and fascinating love, laughter and appreciation are.

For those of you who read forewords, I thought I'd throw in a teaser about what lies ahead in these pages. It's about my dentist. Robin provides his patients with a set of headphones and a radio tuned to a station of their choice. The portable set is placed on the client's lap so they can control the radio. Once they settle in and all that noisy dental machinery is up and running, Robin has a habit of leaning over and yelling, "If the pain gets humanly impossible to stand and totally unbearable, *turn up the volume!*"

Let's turn up the volume on uplifting interaction—and what I mean here is the sheer mass of it.

I would suggest you read the case histories one story at a time, giving yourself the wherewithal to savour and integrate what comes off the pages. You too will notice change in your life. If you don't, others will surely speak up and let you know how, for *some* reason, something has changed about you.

Happy travelling!

John J. Heney
Ottawa, Canada
April 2003

A.
My Card . . .

Allow me to introduce myself. When people ask my wife Kathy what it is that I do, she simply says, "Ask *him*!" Makes a lot of sense.

I call myself a spiritual mechanic. I demonstrate how *thought* and *energy* are used by our society, and how at times it could use a bit of adjustment. Don't we know it.

Aside from the standard postal address, phone number and e-mail address, my business card bears only my name. There's not enough room on it to also print:

Remembering to Play
Couples
Ghosts (See Couples)
Official Grantor of Permission to Play and to Show Your Teenager
How to Do It
Speaking Engagements that Really *Do* Engage
Boss Work (Two Meanings, If You Get My Meaning)
Office Play (See Boss Work)
Inner Work Outreach
Inner Adult Work for Children
How to Outsource Inner Peace
Weirdness Made Practical
How to be an Ogre with Grace
Who Woulda Thunk Thinking
Directing with Your Head, Thinking with Your Tummy

(And How to *Finally* be Able to Tell the Difference)
Making Your Struggle into an Inspiration without Struggling
Applying the Magic of Respect
People Training for Pets
Births that Make Sense, Passages that Inspire and
Everything Else In Between
Becoming the Healer You'd Love to Meet
Interior Decorating for the Walls of Your Box
Common Sense Made Common
Feeling the Feelings
Becoming Sovereign

Working with principles makes things so much easier. Don't you think? Principles seem to have a further reach and a deeper impact than *method*.

We know that between 1644 and 1729 AD, or what is becoming known as the Common Era (CE), people in Europe suspected of being witches were transported to Oudewater, Holland. There they were weighed. Conviction was automatic for any female who weighed in at more than ninety-nine pounds. Men and women died in Europe and America by the thousands in widespread witch scares. It seems backward and destructive to us today, but it was all too real to people living in that era.

So much of that pain could have been and can be prevented when we look at what makes sense. How much energy do societies spend defending "boxes" of belief? Love and compassion, inclusion and fun, help and service can translate into clean water, food on the table, reduced health care costs, cheaper and more widely available goods, cleaner air, and *more*. Part of the answer is to remember how *good* it feels to give ourselves a break and also to have a good time spreading that peaceful feeling. We *seek* simplicity. Have you *felt* it in your life lately?

Such is the nature, then, of what I have come to call spiritual mechanics. When Jesus Christ was quoted as speaking about the power of two or more gathered in His name, what do you think He meant? He was referring to teamwork, and unity and giving and compassion, connection to things seen *and* unseen, and faith. All principles.

My Card

Principles of fun, ease, joy, readiness to learn, and a philosophy of learning that is uplifting, refreshing and forever young are part of it. *Bring* these principles. The techniques you thought you had to master will come. That's because you will be a very attractive source, an *activated* source, of the same light that is within each of us. Forcing it, waiting for it, preaching about it or trying to find it are certain states of being, to be sure. Sharing it is a state of being that moves mountains. As the man we know as Jesus told the world at one time, remember the power and influence of one mustard seed.

Principles of energy that are effective are grounded in the bedrock of respect. Respect for self, respect for others, and respect for all of us. Demonstrating how powerful respect is can be very uplifting, really exciting, and deeply invigorating. Many people look for respect, but often do not find it. Feeling what respect accomplishes can be new for some people who often are not treated with respect; or who may not even have a role model in their lives to show how it functions. As one moves consciously among all manner of energies, bringing respect and demonstrating respect become crucial. Because it can be rare in certain places or circumstances, I carry respect in my back pocket for easy access and regular use.

Being able to jokingly refer to a "business card" like the one above, I help to show people how so many aspects of our lives have more room for common sense, hope, relaxation and unity. As you become even more observant as to how you and others interact, you too will easily spot circumstances where your own reputation with kindness and love can glow and influence.

Before we move on, I would like to ask one small favour.

Each time you finish reading a part of this book, close it and place it between your hands. Hold it for a moment, and think about what you have experienced in its pages. Feel the energy off the book and appreciate that the stories and the lessons have reached just a little bit further in the physical world, and far, *far*—much further indeed—in the world of energy and spirit. You have shared and we have shared and the people profiled here have shared.

Feel it. Get to know the feeling. And pass it on.

Cheers,

John

B.
Coming to Terms with Spirituality And Stepping Up to Bat

You're obviously reading at the same rate that I can type. This is a good thing. As long as I can keep up with your eyes, we'll do just fine. Otherwise you might even get to the end of the book before I do, which would be a feat even Albert Einstein would be proud of.

Barring that occurrence, I can begin by telling you what this book is all about.

After people read my book *The Thunder Within*, some came to me asking about a manual, about more material, about a book that would spell out the principles I described and used when I told my own story. "How," they asked, "can I remember those things that make sense, and use them in my *own* life?"

So, I've come back to the keyboard.

First, if I give the matter some thought, here are some principles I accept.

Wherever I find myself, I also find myself surrounded by energy. So far, that makes me just like you and just like everyone who has ever lived. I live in a "sea of thought" just like you do. One might view it as an ocean of invisible waves that contains *many* vibrations, many beliefs. These include ideas some people have that "the world" is made up of . . .

- Seven days a week
- Three meals a day (even if there is no food to be had, it's the concept)
- Religions that often conduct formal practices between Friday and Sunday

- Kids who are smart and who are taught to shut up
- Adults who would like to be more like kids
- Mass consciousness that differs from place to place about makeup, courting, men, purpose, hierarchy, schooling, and which side of the street to drive on. If you move from Britain to Canada, or the other way around, it is best to keep your awareness on which side of the street you are driving (a very *strong* belief system) and set aside for a moment what you think about men.

Within this "sea of consciousness" each of us glows, each of us has an impact and each of us gives off energy that can be felt or "seen" to varying degrees by other individuals, and which is always felt or seen by the entire cosmos. 'Twas ever thus.

How this energy works seems to have remained constant. *What* we do with it, *what* we get to do with it, and *where* we decide it will take us changes constantly.

The science of what thought and energy really are is catching up to us. Specialists can now watch the brain as a person is excited, elated, worried, occupied or in a dream state during sleep. Thought produces chemical changes, and chemical changes alter thought.

This knowingness is beginning to converge with what we decide to think, making it next to impossible to separate science from the sacred.

If we were to put the science of thought together with the highest intentions of religion, if we were to study ourselves with fascination rather than through judgment or fear, if we embraced the fact that we are all connected and then began to *live* this idea as a scientific truth *as well as* an emotional fact, this sea of consciousness that's around us would experience extraordinary change. And so would we.

In fact, being in contentment, being in pure love, and being in mutual self respect is so foreign to some people that they might even tell you they feel off balance, out of sorts, or strange in some way or another if they began living in it.

A congregation in a temple praying for world peace actually produces an environmental energy. A swarm of teenagers at a rave produces an energy in the vicinity. A schoolteacher berating a child in a way that informs her she will never amount to anything is also an energy, and a professor who imbues his class with hope, inspiration and a sense of service to others also changes the atmosphere.

We are in it, of it, on it, and producers of it. And when the opportunity comes along to enjoy this impact and to get a feel for what it is like to uplift others, things really start to happen. The peace one can find or one can create in a sanctuary need not stay only in the sanctuary. Searches for God need not remain searches. We can give the Guy a break and actually *find* Him. That would make Him *really* happy.

Science has given us an understanding of how sharks sense things in the water through frequencies and vibrations. The side of us that likes to study is also taking steps to more closely understand how soft words and acts of encouragement have an effect on our bodies, on the rooms we inhabit, and on the energy along our congested roadways.

As a species, we have spent *so* much time seeking. Perhaps things would change for the better if more and more of us became finders.

There's an opportunity to pioneer here. It actually can require some courage to slow down and to live with common sense, and to embrace knowingness that is so close to who we really are that often we cannot see it. Like *much* pioneering, there are probably not too many people out there who are prepared to show you the way. It's too new.

Some of the aspects you will find in *Ladies and Gentlemen!* are very old. Some are common, such as "common sense" that in some places is not all *that* common. Some aspects are refreshing, some seem too impossible to be true, and some leave us declaring . . . well . . . "Why didn't *I* think of that!"

In the safety of these pages await stories from outside of you that can lead you *inside*, and give you the courage and motivation to make a difference *exactly where you are*.

Even as the play and fun continue in ways that show people how this is done, the one-on-one and group work I am involved in can spread ever wider and even more quickly through this book you can share with each other, occasionally moving among yourselves to share a "high five" about an uplifting moment.

Enough now about putting fingers to the keyboard.

Frankly, people are just too complicated for words. That's why I work with energy. And *that* affects the self and people. It does not teach or preach, it demonstrates. This moves the talk to the doing, and the study to the graduating. It means creating feelings on the inside rather than just waiting for them to come from the outside.

First let's talk about what it is like to be around people who are open to sharing, and who regularly get a chance to do so as they give themselves permission to play and inspire in the fields of healing, communicating and developing . . .

The question of what constitutes, or does not constitute, spirituality has been haunting humanity for *eons*. Perhaps haunting *is* the correct term to use, because so many people despair that we will ever grasp it. We haven't got a ghost of a chance, they might say. It's a puzzle occupying many planes, many existences. It would do us a world of good if we stopped being so puzzled about it and decided to become fascinated.

If you're out walking in the woods and no one is about, are you being spiritual? Have you noticed that nature has never bothered to stop and to ask a question to which the answer is *soooo* obvious?

Thought is spirituality. Intent is spirituality. Fighting within or outside of one's self is spirituality. Parking your car. Harvesting herbs. Waving at a friend. Attending a staff meeting.

Especially the staff meeting.

Just kidding.

Staff meetings. Perhaps they are symbolic of those times we can slip into believing that spirituality isn't at play there, or that something is missing or that something could be better. The trick is to realize that all the feelings and all the energies and all the expectations and all the thoughts said and unsaid are very much present at a staff meeting, and very much at work, and very real in their impact. Spirituality is *there*.

Perhaps it's easier to discover what spirituality is *not* than to believe you have the whole thing sewn up by declaring what it is.

Look at energy.

Settle yourself for a moment. Find yourself in your imagination. Now, try these out for me:

- Show me the life force—the energy—in and around a person who is worrying about what spirituality is; then,
- Show me the life force of persons who *know* without reservation that they're already swimming in a sea of

thought and energy and that this soup of existence is something they are already influencing just as much as it is influencing them.

Now:
- What differences do you feel between those two people?
- *Who*, exactly, taught them to act the way they are behaving?
- How far does that sort of teaching go back?

We have not, to a large extent as the tribe we are, spent time instructing youngsters how much more free one can be when spirituality is seen as *the very energy we're made of*. Freedom does not mean promiscuity or a lack of responsibility or an absence of ethics. It means freedom from the baggage that comes from worry, being split, "working on" aspects of the self, overcoming or being consumed with envy, jealousy, fear or anger. And it's being free of getting free of those things.

We are the only ones who have the power to decide, for example, that to dispel anger in clean and easy, simple and fast, effective and deep ways is *fun*.

"No 'taint!"
"Yes 'tis."
"Can't be."
"Sure can."
"But *how?*"
"Not how, *why!*"
"What?"

The foregoing conversation was brought to you by spirituality.

That ten seconds *was* spirituality. And it went right by you if it was waiting to be recognized as just that. The two parties engaged in that exchange, be they real people, imagined people, or voices inside you were spiritually churning, changing, affecting, and being felt by energy as much as they were being affected by their own and each other's vibrations.

What we just had there was a spiritual moment.

Noticing such a thing and appreciating these moments are part of what really makes a person a *spiritual mechanic*. That's a person who lives and works and walks and talks in the soup of vibration we live in. They simultaneously appreciate and know this to be a fact even as they marvel at what we do to ourselves and others.

Take a moment to return to that short exchange you just read. Appreciate the changes the mind, the body, and the body/mind were able to make in their perception about what goes on in and around us as we speak. Now do something else . . .

Multiply that exchange by several billion times. The several billions of times such snippets of conversation go on during any given day, all around the world. You begin to get the idea of what we transmit, pick up, and try to let go of, pass around, exchange, slough off, suck in, push through.

I say it's time we declare that, as long as we are going to be doing this all the time, why not give ourselves and our tribe a collective break and begin to have fun, ease, peace and joy with the very forms of communication we've been using consciously and subconsciously for ages?

Who was the first to tame fire? Seems, well, just natural. At least by now.

And who first crossed the Atlantic Ocean—and in *which* direction was that, exactly? Are you *sure*? Who first baked bread? (That's a lot of steps to go through if you stop to think about it!) And who first decided that enough was enough, and they were going to permit that person down the block of a different race/creed/gender/class/education level to get the benefit of his/her smile?

What was spirituality before you got here? And what is it doing now? And what will it be up to after you've gone? So what are you doing with it in the meantime?

Change the world right now, by upgrading your awareness to know that you are always heard, you are always observed, you are always felt, you are always having an impact and you are always influencing something or someone.

No, it's not time to be psychotic. It's time to be naked.

No, it's not time to take your clothes off. It's time to relax.

No, it's not time to fall asleep, it's time to enjoy all the energy you now have that you once were occupying with getting on with getting on, and working out what had to be worked out about yourself and others.

If you don't understand the traditions and manners of your Muslim or Jewish or Christian hosts at the dinner table, *ask*. If they've taken you in, in the midst of a snowstorm when your car broke down, give thanks. Ignorance is an invitation to learn. It is also an opportunity to look like a buffoon, but that's generally not an option I choose and run with.

If you have no appreciation for what older people have been through, *ask*.

If you want to know how much energy you have been using up in old wars, in resentment, and in unresolved matters, sit down. Know that your energy vibrates and is seen. And *ask* how much time and energy is being spent on matters that are not uplifting!

You'll get an answer.

"No I won't"

"Yes y' will."

"Can't do't"

"Ever tried?"

"Never happens."

"Who says? Go ahead."

"You first."

There goes one of them spiritual moments again . . . And the cosmos looks and it shakes its collective head. Two parties, in the foregoing conversation, being spiritual. Again. When will they get the point? There's no *in* of it or *out* of it. It's just what it's *all* about.

Become the first person on the block to fold the idea of spirituality into your entire life and move away from holding it as a separate concept. If you are in a church or synagogue, pray. If you choose to go to a concert, decide on what uplifts people. Smile at a vendor.

One day, I slowly approached a grocery store cashier as the line of customers moved through her station. She was harried, *very* conscientious and moving at a very appreciated lightning speed.

I noticed the coffee, barely touched, that she had near the cash register. I had also observed that she had not touched it for quite a while.

She barely looked up as she began to process my purchases.

"Excuse me," I said, looking right at her.

She didn't look up.

"*Excuse* me!" I said a little more firmly.

That's when she stopped and decided to look up.

I pointed past her to her cup.

"That's been sitting there for quite some time and it's getting cold. It won't hurt me if you pause for a second and take a sip."

She froze.

I had to repeat myself.

She reached back, hardly looking at the coffee, taking it to her lips and having a sip.

"You *wonderful* man!" she exclaimed. "How did you get to be like that? You've made my . . . my *week*! *No one* has ever done that for me before! Thank you *soooo* much! Hey, wow!"

I could not abide the tons of mascara this woman was wearing, which it seemed must have required three hours to apply. I'd noticed this as I had approached her station. Standing there, I decided it would be better for me to look for something else with which to occupy my time.

And that was the result.

If *that* happened everywhere, where would we be? Spirituality is a coffee at the cashier. It's that too.

Before you move on, what are you feeling about the energy off the page? That too is energy, and you too are interacting with it. It's that simple. And it is happening *all* the time.

C.
When Talking It Becomes Living It

If those who are secretly—*deep* inside—going around saying, "Nobody understands me!" suddenly got the chance to be accepted for *exactly* who they are and *exactly* how they feel, what would happen? What would happen if a psychic working day after day with "dark energy" around people got permission to *bring out* the light that happens to be hiding in them, instead of concentrating on the heavy stuff? What if doctors could talk about the energy in their offices, how it changes and shifts; and could appreciate how a cleansing in the atmosphere would perk up the energy in a place the practitioners have to occupy for so many hours?

What would happen if moms stayed in tune with the unseen senses their children feel and express, while helping their youngsters to fully grasp the abilities they have and permitting them to hold on to those abilities through adulthood?

What would happen if people young and old could share, with no fear of reproach, what it is they sense on the bus, see in the night, or feel as they walk past a certain office or cubicle?

They would be practising what they already know. *Presto chango*, their fear of the unknown would disappear. They would be *bringing into* situations that for which they had formerly been *looking*, and the atmosphere would change accordingly.

What if getting spirituality into the workplace became a sensation of *finding it* in the workplace? What if thousands of people on a slogging, hardscrabble, judgmental, recovery-based path took off the yoke of hardship and were able to glide through the marketplace demonstrating how easy it is to show each other how freely we can live with a healthy sense of responsibility and joy?

What if people who secretly long to develop "healing abilities" or capabilities to "see energies and spirit" gave themselves a break? What if they began to realize that enjoying what one has and becoming a teacher as well as a student starts to change the energy to an exciting, satisfied vibration in which greater things happen faster?

What if people began to feel that uplifting the self and uplifting others creates a momentum that rises above the self-recrimination we tend to practise?

Where do people have a chance to do all of this, and to *feel* this, and to demonstrate this?

That's why I have developed the groups I invite people to participate in, wherein I act as a moderator in an open and responsible sharing of thoughts about energy.

As I wandered the marketplace of healing possibilities myself—something I recounted in my book *The Thunder Within*—I noticed there were all manner of approaches to healing: treating the body and mind with bodywork, breathing, various therapies, applied products, ingested products, acupuncture, and so on.

By seeing what I saw, I noticed what was missing. What did not seem to be available was a healthy, respectful venue where people could, with fun and joy, take a look at how they were looking at things, and take a look at how fast they could relieve themselves of baggage they did not actually have to carry or work through.

Nowhere did I see an environment where young and old could take a look at how we learned to learn or were taught to teach, and how really outmoded or inaccurate or ineffective and cumbersome many of these "tribal practices" are.

Nowhere did I come across venues where healing was considered fascinating and fun, and that by working in loving ways with the self and others, a momentum could build that would vibrate in such a way as to give other people hope and *permission* to lighten up and serve others even as they brought themselves into more balance.

Nowhere did I encounter a forum for exchange in which people could bring to the table aspects of their life that, during the week, had raised a question, twigged a fear, opened an opportunity, or brought a problem they wanted to share or ask about without fear of feeling out of place, foolish or inadequate.

And I did not come across a place where people actually addressing an aspect of their lives could be with others who were not tying them down to that aspect, or miring them in victimhood, hopelessness, or a sense of identification that inhibited growth.

So, slowly at first, I established such a meeting opportunity.

Other than a chance to practise common sense, I really have no name for it.

That's what people experience when they attend the sessions I host. They're two hours or so in duration, most often in the evening. It's not therapy, although aspects of *who people are* do change in these experiences. We don't scream or throw things. We take the time to look at the wisdom we can use when we look at things, and we give people the chance to practise so they can feel the lightness and joy that come with common sense, so that the vibration this atmosphere gives off can be encouraged and broadcast.

It's simple in its concept and, from what I have experienced, widely sought after. Not many people know about it, and in my experience, not many people have dared to establish it. The longing for a refreshing approach simmers in a very quiet, underground way. Sometimes the mere thought that such groups exist is far from a person's sense of the possible.

Scratch an individual and underneath you will probably find someone rolling his eyes about what he is dealing with or how people are interacting with him in debilitating ways. Yet he does not dare act to show the alternative—show how things *could* be.

So, meeting to experience the mechanics of how thought and energy function is to cross a bridge. That's when talking about what works and what makes sense becomes living it.

It means that church ministers who are in formal positions of leadership and example can let their hair down about the pressures there can be in living in such a role. Parents can let themselves realize that they really *do* have the same senses their children possess and as adults they can remember how to communicate with *all* their abilities even though their own society taught them to forget these natural gifts—which we often call supernatural, rare, or unattainable.

The level of comfort in the environment of groups such as the one I am describing is not just something attained; it is something one can teach by example.

I often joke that people might better be taught to work with *energy*, and *not* with people, for people are *so* complicated, *so* mixed up, *so* set in their ways, *so* blinded by traditions and *so* apt to make things tough or screw things up that they should well be left alone.

I have never had the experience of someone disagreeing with me on that one. The realization of "energy, not people" is observing the obvious. By embracing universal truths, we prove also ready to step back from other things that, for the longest time, did not work for us and did not make any sense to the person we really knew ourselves to be all along.

That's why so many adults can remember as children times when they *knew* that what was going on was not reflecting the truth, and they *knew* that certain imposed rules were not actually effective in bringing about peace, co-operation, and enhancement. The Biblical commandment "Thou shalt not kill" makes great socioeconomic sense to most people, but better it should be taught as, "Respect all life." The difference one gets at the pit of the stomach off these two rules seems to be universal. The latter one uplifts and includes, the former admonishes and restricts. The latter is easier to teach and, if widely used, would be easier to maintain, too.

Some Thoughts:

1. If it is true that we often find other people's phobias, blockages, limitations and relationship muck-ups fascinating, it stands to reason that our own can be just as interesting to other people. Since it is true that humans are so exquisite at creating drama, why not dare to become fascinated by what we build, and then continue to build, rather than getting into a rant about what has not worked.

2. The energy and the actual physical body of a person does pick up the intent of people around them. A touch that is caring feels a lot different than a touch that's controlling. This being the case, bring the energies you would like to see and feel around you, and teach what they can do. This is why what is spoken in the room, for example, when

people are medically operating on a person, is of paramount importance. All energy is present, and the patient is very much present indeed. Know it.

3. Wanting to "develop" but not giving yourself the chance to graduate only helps to guarantee we will be stuck with a bunch of students who never advance. Many teachers will tell you that the most simple of principles are often the hardest to teach. This leads some to put gurus on higher and higher pedestals (and for some gurus to place themselves there!). We already know. Many are afraid to practise.

4. Giving yourself a break about "issues" you have been working on takes what I call "bold humility." Bold in that you have the audacity to declare you are tired of struggle, and humility to know that you are not alone, you do not know everything, and that the presence of a higher force, being, God, Creator, etc. is an asset, not a hindrance. It's a relaxing recognition. "God knows" we have been struggling over things for a long time, and that commandments directing us to "Respect All Life" would probably go further than reminding us that "Thou Shalt Not Kill."

5. If you would like to see joyous, uplifting energy, where are you going to find it? Why not bring it to others and "Become the Person You'd Love to Meet."

These are just some of the things we discuss and practise when we get together with people from all walks of life who are ready to say, "There's a lot more we could be doing and there are better things to do than to wallow in struggle. We have to get on with realizing how great and powerful we are and that power is not a positioning, it is a blossoming."

By meeting as we do, we know that the energy glows and broadcasts, giving hope and love to all around us, not in saving and salvation, but in demonstrating and teaching. From such interaction, and from such work, come experiences the likes of which you will find in the pages of this book. Now, on to some of those adventures . . .

D.
A Treasury of Case Histories And Other Observations

1. Walking Around the Hurdles

Before looking at how energy functions, let's get some of the big stuff out of the way. Often, what people end up struggling with is not the issue at hand. They're actually fighting with the belief *underneath* the issue. Often it is not a belief such as, "I'll never be able to do this!" but the view of the world that lies below that. The belief itself is content. How the belief got there and how it is extracted or changed goes a bit deeper, and is all about method. What makes these beliefs work in the first place is deeper still, and is all about universal principles of energy. The deeper the work, the more profound the effect, and the greater the amount of time and energy saved.

"My ego's getting in the way."

Now that's a piece of content if I ever heard one! A superb idea. A fabulous notion indeed. Now tell me again: Who taught you that you that you have an ego? Find me a newborn baby who even gives a poop about the fact you have one. (Giving a poop might be about all the kid desires to do anyway.) Baby wouldn't even know an ego if it changed her diapers.

Deeper level now. Who told you that egos get in the way? How often? How fast? From what direction? With what intent? That's all method. Want more method? How do you stop your ego from getting in the way? Will it come back? Does it care? That's all method.

Deeper still. Who told you you had to work on your ego? Who told you you needed to address it? Couldn't you be baking a cake, digging in your garden, telephoning a shut-in? The very statement that we started with here set up a whole piece of work.

If you had never heard the word "ego" would you know to work on it? Could you struggle with it if you didn't know it existed? Does it actually feel *good* to get the ego out of the way before you do something? What more could you accomplish if you were not occupying your time struggling with it?

What would your tribe do if you were to announce you don't have an ego? Would you be stoned to death? What would your tribe do if you announced that you have given up feeding your ego, not feeding it, getting it out of the way, watching for it, denying it, and the like?

How do you feel about that idea? Feeling fed up with struggling seems to be a universal phenomenon. Incidents of people deciding they do not need to struggle seem a bit rare. Even more exquisite is the decision to have fun. It's about daring to show how care and strife can be sloughed off and replaced with something uplifting, something joyous, something expansive.

Now, go and interview a newborn baby. (Please see important footnote below.)[1]

Find out from the youngster how much he has not yet been taught that he will find himself having to un-think, work on, get over, let go of, and so on. Say a prayer.

Prayers are strong and very real declarations. Use one to announce to the universe that here is a child who, through contact with another soul—yourself—has had a very real and deep energy exchange. Declare that this has put a stop to so much of the stuff we work through that does not have to be worked through. Mean it and it is done.

---

[1] Generally it is good to interview newborn babies when no one is watching. The baby might get embarrassed. Until it becomes common practice, you may be questioned about what you are doing. Nonetheless, do it for yourself, and for heaven's sake do it for the baby! Give the toddler a real *feel* for what it is like to be in the presence of a "big person" with few hang-ups. It brings them hope for the future. Give their "inner child" a break right from the start, and do all of us a great favour.

With this exercise you are extending to your tribe the knowledge that energy follows intent, and that life in its continuation can make improvements and progress. In giving the baby that which you might have liked given to you and done with you when you were young, you are in a more forgiving state about certain practices that, although perhaps well-meaning, ended up stifling your energy and beliefs. Now you are passing on a greater wisdom, and giving credit to yourself for fully participating in how we create our social fabric. You are actually *living* the fact that you have an impact, and you may be switching from reacting *to* energy to creating *with* it.

One might as well call this aspect of the principles of energy "Walking Around the Hurdles." The option is often right in front of your face. It's so easy it can seem impossible. But it's one of those times when it's okay to exclaim, "Why didn't *I* think of that!"

After watching people bang their heads against issues, and perhaps doing it enough yourself so that the idea of stopping becomes painful in itself, it might be wise—indeed, exciting—to see what happens when we no longer struggle. It's thrilling to surprise the universe with the gift of someone who finally gets it—that we are all creators of drama and "boxes." As long as we are, we might as well have fun with it and go back to the notion of play, even the play that so many adults tell me they would love to be able to do again but were never given permission to do, and perhaps even forcibly restricted from experiencing.

Some Thoughts:

1. We really are too hard on ourselves. When you have fun discovering how we do this, you may be surprised as often as you also *become* a surprise to others. You may also be astonished when you realize how much energy we spend on struggle, how much we really thought was deep feels insignificant now, and how much you can begin to feel you are an example that is actually showing others that release and relief need not be expensive, drawn out, complicated or painful.

2. You want to play? Bring play. Cease waiting for play to come to you, and dare to bring it. That's the fastest way to have it around.
3. Begin to be fascinated by what we, as a "tribe," say and do. For example, notice people's restricting or enhancing speech patterns. Become curious about these rather than judgmental. As for you, take a breather. Once you have congratulated yourself on what you have built, become as an artisan. Develop *additional* uplifting processes. That way, the world inherits one more person at play who uplifts the energy wherever he or she happens to be.

2. Stop Stopping Doing This!

An approach on behalf of . . .

It's a phrase many of us say to ourselves often enough. It goes, *"I've got to stop doing this."*
There are many variations:
"I've got to stop forgetting to remind myself to stop doing this."
"I keep slipping up."
"I keep sliding into old habits."
And so on.
Do you know anyone who engages in this behaviour?
Don't be shy! I'm sure you can think of *someone*. Let's suppose ("I have this friend, see . . .") that someone came to you begging to be shown how to be released from the entanglements and traps these statements create. It's as if they *want* to be free of the struggle, but believe they won't be free until they're free of it. How would you advise them? How about we prepare you for just such an eventuality? For your friend, I mean.
Take another look.

Suppose you could float above your city, or the region you live in, and have a green light appear above the head of every individual who is busily engaged in that ages-old pastime, trying to stop doing something. Wouldn't the sky light up! Certainly would! I call this observation, "turning on the beacons." Make a note of it. And use it.

Our tribe is full of examples of how we've taught ourselves and others to make changes by kicking a habit or getting off something. Even when we try *not* to try, it's difficult.

Whether the subject be smoking or temper or weight loss or exercise or not forgetting, or even if it's about remembering, things get fouled up. Chances are there is at least *one* person around who is working on the same problem.

Move outside of your own concerns, and do something for *them*. Serve your fellow sufferers (*oops, did I let something slip there?*). One of the greatest ways to get yourself out of a rut is to do something kind for another person. And if you start with the topic at hand, you don't even have to worry about moving on the chessboard! You begin to learn right where you are. It should be so easy.

Suppose someone in this sea of individuals is working at trying to do something *and she actually succeeds!* And she had *fun* with it? What would *that* do?

Wouldn't it raise the possibility of it being done again?

Wouldn't it set an example?

Wouldn't it inspire?

Would it make her a leader rather than a pusher or a person who shoves herself toward change?

It's all energy. *You* might as well act on behalf of all these poor souls. And on behalf of humanity, and on behalf of yourself and on behalf of people who were not taught anything better.

In the chapter called "Listen Up!" we disclose the power of the declaration. Let's try one here. How about reading this one out loud?

Ladies and Gentlemen!

On behalf of all people who are trying to stop smoking, I would like to demonstrate to you what happens to my body when I become fascinated with the whole idea of smoking and how it works. I'm an individual, and because I respect myself as a unique person, there are likely unique reasons as well as common reasons why I started to smoke in the first place. As I know what it feels like to smoke and I know what it feels like to want to stop smoking, I want you to know that in addition to helping me, this is going to help all others in my position. It takes one to know one, and boy, do I know one! As this uplifting strategy grows, it can move to other subjects for people who are trying to stop this or that or whatever. And it starts here.

I'm going to move from the symptoms to the causes. And now I'm going to move from the causes to the benefits of learning something new.

Who says I need to do all the work? What about the energy around me? If the energy around me is affected by smoking, why can't the energy around me change in such a way that it no longer needs smoking? I'm going to look at the energy one metre around me and speak to it about what it can do, now that it is no longer occupied with smoking. And then I'm going to ask it to go and tell the energy around other smokers what can be done more easily.

Look at my tummy. See how it's relaxing more? And notice how it is letting in more oxygen so that I am more invigorated so that I no longer need to pump myself up with nicotine? That's it for now. Thanks for listening, and please celebrate that you have been around someone changing energy in a joyous way. Talk to you later.

You have just become, in the same instant, a teacher, an inspiration and a leader. You're a person who is being more kind to yourself and your body. You're learning, but you are *also* declaring. And you are appreciating that all energy *is* energy and that all thought has an effect. How do you feel? How does the energy around you feel *now*?

Some Thoughts:

1. It's okay to admit that you're not having fun if the job is too hard. You won't lose points.
2. It's okay to admit that part of the strain is what is taking place in your body because you feel it is an uphill battle.
3. It's okay to admit that your thoughts and intentions have an immediate effect on the surrounding atmosphere.
4. It's okay to admit you have leadership qualities.

In 1899, Charles H. Duell, the U.S. commissioner of patents, declared that everything that could be invented had already been invented by then. *Hmpgh*! Since we now know that not to be true, what else can be invented? And are you not right now inventing how you invent change for yourself? Like radio, television and hand-held computers, this too might someday be commonplace, but all of this at one time or another had to be invented. You have stepped up to join the ranks of the inspired. Not bad.

I once had occasion to sit with a couple who had come with individual and very personal challenges. After they'd calmly stated their respective cases, I asked the woman to stand in front of me. With her permission, I gently touched her here and there with my finger as I had her repeat declarations much as the one you just finished reading, only tailored to her life and conundrums. She gave her tummy back to her tummy, no longer treating it as a repository of stress or problems, and changed her tack from overcoming and being challenged, to inspiring and demonstrating self-caring so others could *learn by example*. She felt immediate changes in her body and around her. She was amazed at the speed and ease of the change.

"What am I supposed to do to help her in this? What can I do?" asked her husband.

"Become the world's first couple that *stops stopping doing things* together, for yourself and for each other and on behalf of all men and all women and all couples *and* all households. Simply show how it is done, and laugh with yourselves along the way," I replied.

We had a fun-filled session.

Toward the end of the visit, the husband declared about some aspect of his life, "I'm going to have to work on that one!"

"*No!*" declared his wife as she sat right beside him on the couch "We're going to show how play *replaces* work!" And as *this* relationship between persons, who happen to be in their sixties, begins to demonstrate, couples young and old can get the point, by example.

They certainly left uplifted, in a space for more humour, and being more gentle with themselves and each other. Changing the approach had moved faster than tackling the issue.

Some More Thoughts:

1. If it's a struggle, it's probably a struggle. Decide to do it differently.

2. Serve others like you when you change yourself. You'll be surprised how much lighter the transition seems.

3. Ask the question, "Who taught me to think that way?" And then ask, "Who taught them?" And then again, "Who taught *them*?" Sit in a bathtub. (Undress first. Fill the tub with warm water. *Then* sit in it.) Then ask yourself that question. Over and over again. Until you get the point.

3. Listen Up!

The Gospel of John opens with the reminder that, as far as the cosmos goes, "In the beginning was the word." To speak is to emphasize that energy follows intent. That's why I often ask people to make declarations out loud when they have intentions, and to become fascinated and self-empowering as they do it. Part of speaking out is about making change, but part of it is to build an understanding of and a comfort with something that can be a tool for the rest of your life.

Sometimes it helps to hear about something being done before embarking upon it yourself. A man who had been a client of mine told me how his thirteen-year-old son had piped up one day and declared that he wanted to meet me, with the intention of sharing and having some time alone. A few months passed, and I received an e-mail from this very polite and sincere young man who hoped his approach wasn't going to be taken as too forward. He wrote:

> I finally have a chance to write you J, I've been meaning to write you because my life is messed. I don't really know if you

can help but you're the only person I can think of to write to right now. I've heard you do some really amazing things, one of my goals in life are to be able to have that ability active, its just I feel like I have a lack of will. Heh, I bet this email seems sort of abrupt and I'm asking you to help, when I don't even know you, anyway try and write back if you can sometime, and I will reply to those emails as fast as possible.

We began an e-mail exchange.

First, I demonstrated to him the Art of the Declaration. I wrote him an example. I suggested how it's a good idea to begin these declarations with the words, "*Ladies and Gentlemen!*" This shows how one is inclusive, polite in all circumstances, unconcerned about who's listening because the intent is clear and uplifting, and willing to set an example about how things can be accomplished.

I asked him to read the e-mail to himself, and then to read it out loud. I asked him to take note of what he was feeling during and after reading it. I asked him to take note of changes in the feeling around him and in the room. Fact is, I told him, this is so easy, it's not work at all. Sometimes, I said in my e-mail, for me it's about talking straight out. I asked him to read the next paragraph and then to stop for a pause after he had finished. Find out what it feels like to read the paragraph, and then read it out loud if you can where you are. Here's what I asked him to read silently and then out loud:

Ladies and Gentlemen:

My name is ——— and I'm open for business. I wish to use my abilities to serve others for their highest good. And I would like to show the world how peace, fun and joy in one's walk changes the energy around a person and through his life. It's going to be fascinating to be able to show the world how people can live together and work together without fuss. I know it feels strange at times being "the first kid on the block" to do this, but there will be others and I will be able to show them how things work. As for my connecting with John, he and I will be able to show how respect in learning about energy can move things really fast. And about that thing of people controlling me or using their energy in such a way. That is a very old and boring way to use energy, but something they are used to because they have not learned about uplifting living with thought. So I'm going to show you what happens when I peacefully acknowledge this and live my day using my aura to show a new approach. Thanks for listening. (Signed) ⸺.

He wrote back:

That paragraph was . . . inspiring, what I "want" to be in life right now. Amazing, wow, zam, pow, astounding, astonishing . . . the list goes on. That paragraph really does "get my energy out of a rut." I understand the "stopping" comment, it makes sense, if I'm trying to change this, I don't try and stop this. I very much enjoy talking with you, and look forward to your next email, your advice seems to be just what I need.

The next step was to have him try this on his own. I asked him if I could have his permission to read this to one of the groups I meet with to discuss energy and how it functions. He was more than willing, and in fact pleased that he could contribute. The energy off the letter impressed those who heard it. Here's what he wrote:

Ladies and Gentlemen:

Working with John is creating growth in me by helping me begin a spiritual journey. When people work together, the combined energies are more powerful, and will help me more on my journey. I feel that John will teach me a lot about energy, myself, and the world around me and that he will help me get out of my energy rut. John helping me will add his energies to mine, and this is important to not lead me on a strange path. After the shock of seeing this strange occurrence, kids my age might be scared, frightened or even interested. Some will think this is insane, but the seed will be planted and someday it will be normal for them, some others will want to learn, and hopefully I will be able to teach them with all I learn from John. When older people see this relationship of learning, they will discover that anyone can learn, and has the opportunity and power to change any aspect of their lives. This is one of the most important lessons to learn in life, and hopefully this will help them achieve it.

Because I'm young, I do not have all the impressions of the world on me, I have grown up about this idea, and the energies are around me, they just need to be enhanced. Some other people will have difficulty living in this style, but the younger ones will be easier to teach. Also John's energies can help me learn about energy and life, easier than all alone.

Not bad for a thirteen-year-old. In fact, to be *that* age when one begins to have fun again with energy is a real blessing. To begin again at any age is wondrous. In fact, when you work with as many ghosts as I have, you get to know how often people at *all* levels of existence slap themselves on the brow and declare, "Wow! Why didn't *I* think of that! It's so *simple!*"

The young man composed the letter, and then read it. "When I read this the first time (just in my head) it seemed 'technical' somehow, and I don't think that is how this should be. I guess that tingly 'neat' feeling felt like it was coming from me somehow. I don't know if this will change when I read it out loud, but I will when I have the chance."

And he subsequently reported: "When I read this the second time it was out loud, and felt the same, just more powerful. Also, now it felt like the energy was infusing me, but also 'swirling' around me. Pretty cool."

Letters and declarations of intent that are uplifting, inspirational, inclusive, connected and inspiring can change a person and an environment. Sharing a positive outlook is a lot easier than keeping or sustaining one.

Some Thoughts:

1. Give others at every turn a helping hand in remembering who we are and how we create.
2. Celebrate opening up and returning to creativity wherever you are and at whatever age you happen to be.
3. Put into practice your God-given ability to create change. Don't *wait* for joy, *bring* it.
4. Energy follows intent. A thought is an energy. To speak it is to give it life and direction. To speak it is to give it the force and backing of action.

5. Among the things that strengthen what you say are making declarations that include helping others and making declarations that state clearly how positive aspects are true and are already operating.

6. No level of understanding or preparation is needed for this. Just do it.

4. Being There

Being There was a popular 1979 movie starring Peter Sellers based on the novel of the same name by Jerzy Kosinski. Sellers played the part of a simple gardener whose naïve wisdom drew the rich and powerful to seek his counsel. It was at once a fable reminding us about the impact of simplicity, and about the knots we tie ourselves in over controlling life and our journeys.

The movie underlined just how uncomplicated a joyous life can be. Moving it from the wide screen to your own life can seem to be difficult at times. But in fact it can be a lot of fun.

I once got a call from Marty, a man in his early twenties who worked with one of the participants in my groups. He was curious, eager and polite during our initial phone chat, and subsequently came to the group. His questions were universal ones, wise and useful, concerning the kinds of topics we could all use a refresher on.

What about his fear?

What about his ability to retain what he learned that night?

What about his behaviour when he was in the presence of people more advanced than he, or less advanced than he?

What about his struggle to understand?

As I often say, I invited him to move from talking about these things, to *doing*.

I asked Marty to settle himself in a chair, with legs uncrossed, and to simply repeat after me. Here's what he ended up declaring. Read this out loud yourself and see what happens:

Ladies and Gentlemen!

I would like to show you what happens to people's bodies when they decide, as I have, to drop the idea of working about fear, over fear, through fear, and in spite of fear. Look at this! Feel what's happening. Isn't this great!

It's about time someone actually showed everyone how this works. Energy follows intent. As for meeting advanced people, those who are really advanced don't care a hoot about being advanced. Those who are advanced celebrate the advancement of others. The more advanced, the less one has advancement on one's mind. The thought is about inspiration.

Can you see what is happening to me? This is really cool! And look at the energy in the room, and take a look at the energy among the people gathered here in a circle. Notice there is no judgment about where I am at, or what I am about. Look at the wider spaces made available for growth and sharing and how we are right now living and demonstrating how things can be. So, ladies and gentlemen, I am a teaching student and a studious teacher. I am serving everyone here even as I am served. Please take this with you and show others, so that they can save time as well. Thank you very much.

I would like you to take a breath. How do you feel?

Now, just as Marty did, check the energy about a metre (three feet or so) around you. What do you feel? I asked that young man to do the same. What *did* Marty feel? He was amazed at the transformation, the peace within and around him, the expansion of space around him. He reported feeling wrapped in calm, with his shoulders more relaxed and weight taken from his body.

"How did you DO that?" he exclaimed to me. "Wow!"

"He didn't do anything," explained one of the other group members. "*You* did that."

As with many aspects of how we work with thought and energy, the proof of something is in the doing of it, and the doing of something creates a chain reaction that provides the proof. Although this was new for Marty, as it may be for you, each of you has actually done the exercise of making a declaration.

Some Thoughts:

1. Deciding you are going to work on something is a thought and an energy. Shifting your focus to things more enhancing, more uplifting and more inspiring changes the energy.

2. If you were to illuminate a small green light above the head of everyone secretly or publicly "working on something," or trying to "get over something," how bright would the sky become?

3. Beginning your declarations with *"Ladies and Gentlemen!"* tells the universe that you know and accept that:

    - you are not alone

    - there is more to the cosmos and life than you are aware of

    - you treat all energies and beings and persons with respect

    - you feel and acknowledge connection with all things

    - you know you are not alone in believing or having been taught that you have to struggle and at some level you acknowledge you are exhausted by that

    - you live a life in service of others—and that serves you

    - you have a sense of humour in realizing, with a wink, that to work with energy is far easier than working with people, for people are *so* complicated and, at times, *soooo* troublesome.

4. Faith is commendable; knowingness is being there. Having faith that your words matter and create vibration and change is one thing. Knowing at a deep level that they

actually do so settles your "system"—body, mind and soul—even more deeply. You matter. Your words matter. Speaking your thoughts out loud adds action—the physical movement of your throat, tongue and mouth—making your idea stronger. The very vibration itself means that the thought is heard, and that, too, travels to people and in directions many are only just beginning to understand.

5. Ironing Things Out

She was the sister of a client who was the friend of an acquaintance who happened to know what I do. Just like so many people who come to see me. Yes, she and I spent some of the session unravelling many tribally taught tangles and torments. We also turned to a serious and pressing challenge in this woman's life.

Her husband, it seemed, was an alcoholic. Her friends, she said, were telling her that she didn't deserve this. Some of them, anyway. Others were declaring that she must have done something to deserve this. And she was beating herself over the head about having created it, and feeling helpless about doing something about it.

"You like to iron, don't you?" I said.

They just come, these pronouncements I make at times. They just come. It's not practised or a miracle. It's just an approach. It's *The Cleanest, Most Simple, Most Uplifting and Joyous, Inspirational and Easy-on-the-System Way of Doing Things (Inc.)*. You might say it's projected thought out, returned thought in.

How does that work?

Well . . .

It's The Cleanest, Most Simple, Most Uplifting and Joyous, Inspirational and Easy-on-the-System Way of Doing Things (Inc.). But that's another chapter. (By repeating this again, and again, one can get the point across eventually.)

"Yes, I do," she replied about the ironing.

I could tell, in the ensuing millisecond, that she had nonetheless failed to iron out what the connection was. So I explained.

"Suppose you were an alcoholic. And at some level you knew that you knew that it wasn't good for you. Or that you shouldn't be doing it. Or that it was bunging up your life or the lives of those around you."

She absorbed the thought.

Cells in the body aren't stupid (they may be programmed, but they're *not* stupid). They *consciously* pick up the feel in a room, the atmosphere of a conversation, the intent of a bystander, the emotions of a spouse. They feel the recognition of a rut even though they may not want to get out of it. And they hold certain things to be true and *inviolate*, which is a fancy word that means "kept sacred" or "unbroken." (Try telling your boss that certain of your expectations are *inviolate*. Then call me.)

People's cells feel what they are doing. And they feel what others are feeling. And they're looking for a "way out" or a change but have been conditioned to see change as difficult or familiar ways as too comfortable. "They" are not ready to be creative, and "others" are not bold enough to do so as well.

Ever try to be non-judgmental? Then do you find yourself actually judging yourself about how non-judgmental you are or ought to be? Go chase your tail. (At least the neighbours will get a laugh out of it.) The alcoholic is us, and we are the alcoholic. And if it isn't our alcoholism it's our smoking or our diet or our expectations vs. our output. You too could be the first kid on the block to stop stopping. If you would like him to stop stopping, then the first person you need to be kind to is yourself. If you happen to be involved, if you happen to be around and if it happens not to be possible to extricate yourself from the scene, what do you do?

Become creative.

"Do you iron most of your husband's things?" I continued on my track.

"Yes."

"And since all energy is energy, would it not stand to reason that your intent would be felt?"

"Yes."

"And could it not be true that by ironing and feeling you were having an effect and becoming relaxed and studying about how we all affect each other and giving the guilty and grieving parts of your spouse a rest, you would feel better?"

She could hardly wait to get ironing. Like so many of us, she had been hard on herself for finding herself in a difficult circumstance, and hard on her husband; and also, like so many of us, without the training we could use about how easy it is to bring positive energy.

Some Thoughts:

1. It is not that we can or should try to change or understand or logically come to grips with all that each of us is. Part of us is a taxpayer, part of us may abuse substances. Part of us laughs at comedy and part of us deals with grief. Part of us may want to be a parent, and part of us might have to deal with the delivery of a challenged child.

2. As long as we are in the game, it takes nothing to stretch out a hand. And it means everything to do so. At times it is not about *working* on anything, be it alcoholism or internal turmoil around why one married an alcoholic, but to give room for release and relief.

3. Although this woman lived far from my home and I have not seen or heard from her for years, I could tell that the effect of even this one sharing had a deep effect. As with many cases, I took the time to bring similar light into other aspects of her life, leaving her, as she made me fully aware at the time, with renewed energy and hope. Trying to iron things out can really be a chore. Deciding to bring inspiration to the fact that we are all connected takes the creases out of many a fabric.

6. Childhood Issues in Iceland (And Other Obstacles)

This story will greatly benefit people from Iceland, so go fetch one. (Of course, some might assume right away that, this being the case, it's best to turn the page and move on. Off they go to the next chapter. Let's you and I continue.)

What happened in order to create *this* section of the book gave me the chuckles for a few weeks. At least. At the same time, the following exchange brought relief to the gal who was kind enough to bring childhood issues in Iceland to my undivided attention.

"I'm working on my childhood issues," this normally bright and cheerful young lady confessed to me after booking an appointment. She seemed at the end of her rope. By merely looking at her face, one could tell that the subject matter, not to mention dealing with it, was not bringing much joy.

"*Wow!*" I exclaimed, thumping the arm of my chair, now full of new hope, a deeper inner peace and increased vigour. "You mean that even in one of the most remote parts of the planet, surrounded entirely by the Atlantic Ocean, and so named because it hasn't the most hospitable geology and climate—even *there*—they have childhood issues?"

Just like the rest of us! Clearly, I advised her, she had come with one of two messages. Either there's no hope for *anyone* now, *or* we can all heave a sigh of relief that—as long as it's certain there's *no* place to hide—we might as well give up and relax!

My guest was unable to keep a straight face.

"Wait till I tell people they can all relax now!" I continued. "We can all lock up and go home!"

I asked her if she wanted to trade. I was sure I could *easily* solve five Icelandic childhood issues for every one she could wipe out for a Canadian. I asked her if she was familiar with *Canadian* childhood issues. Man, Canadian issues! (Don't go there, man, you'll *never* get out! Keep reading!)

Why does the mere notion of trading issues bring laughter? The idea is part of a universal truth that rings within all of us. We're schooled consciously and subconsciously to look for others' shortcomings while hiding our own, or to work hard on ourselves while scheming to handle those of others. Our worlds within and without can easily become stale and lifeless this way.

Perhaps that's why so many people speak so disparagingly about housework. It's so repetitive, so familiar, and so regular in its demands. A physical manifestation of inner drudgery.

Housework takes many forms (or lack of form, some might say, visualizing their dwelling place). Being a more or less universal thing, the very tradition called "housework" presents an opportunity to bring a new perspective. Let's take a closer look . . .

Funny things happen inside many people when I apply the idea of housework to illustrate a possible new approach to childhood issues. Consider this:

Gather a group of your friends. Put your names in a hat. Have each of you draw one out. This coming Saturday, coordinate it so that each of you arrives at the respective homes in such a way that each one ends up cleaning someone *else's* abode. Some possible results:

- the work would be done faster
- many people would clean up during the week for the cleaners
- more work would be done on the whole
- participants would feel more invigorated.

A couple of things begin to happen. Some people would find themselves exhilarated and even energized at the end of the day. Others would have the cleanest residences on the block because they would toil all week to prepare their home for the arrival of the cleaners, not wanting to look like a slob. In any event, the idea always draws a reaction.

It's amazing what happens to the faces in a crowd when I suggest this to a gathering. So it is with the same boring issues we may find ourselves faced with. It's just too hard or too boring to do the same old thing. We not only get caught up in the doing, we get caught up in the familiarity of it all. And we can become obsessed with the guilt just like we do sometimes with housework.

Sometimes a whole new look at things and why you are doing them can make all the difference in the world. Housework can mean appreciating what it is you have. Don't like cleaning the toilet? Do without one. Hate to clean the sink? Who needs hot and cold running water?

Why can we laugh about housework? Most of us have to do it in some form or another. And most of us have found ourselves at some level speaking of *inner housework* we believe we have to do or are told we have to do.

What would happen if someone got into your shoes, got the feeling for, say, your fear of heights, and gave you a fresh perspective that at least would calm you down? What if someone else lived with that crusty relative instead of you? What if someone with no ties to that ex-boyfriend took a look and got a feel for that relationship?

Expand your purpose! On a personal level, are you getting over an addiction? Are you reinventing yourself? Are you getting out of a rut? Then do it for others, not just for yourself.

Go trade childhood issues and see what happens. Have someone describe it. Imagine yourself walking into that space in someone's story with your fresh perspective, bringing new ideas. We can all be light on our feet in someone else's family, in someone else's schoolyard, on someone else's team.

Have someone *else* imagine herself in your shoes and have her come up with new reactions. How does it feel?

Know what? Part of the glue that keeps problems together is that we think—or we think that we think—that we're all alone in this; or even if we appreciate that others can have the same problem, we feel isolated in the solution. What's more, when people with entirely different challenges come together to do this—let's say over a fear of dogs, or trouble with alcohol that is said to go back to childhood experiences, or a fear of heights or trouble speaking in public—it becomes quite a hilarious parlour game.

Something else happens. The energy in the room actually changes. Energy around the participants takes on a whole new team meaning. Ideas take on a "what if" flavour, and as the level of fascination rises about what we have each been through as a patchwork quilt of experience, the level of judgment on the self and others goes down. It's not about confession or exposure or judgment, it's about setting a new example and daring to do it in *your* living room (of all places!).

What happens when you suggest to someone that he work on one of your issues? *Who woulda thunk?* Try it out.

Doing the thing and getting the feeling. That's what it's all about.

A good friend of mine found herself in a position of having promised her eleven-year-old son who wanted to go skydiving that she would accompany him in doing so on his eighteenth birthday. Darned if this forty-something single mother didn't pull it off! And she ended up, seven years after the promise had been made, jumping first. Once you've done *that*, you sure have the feeling.

Now, helping someone with a childhood issue by showing him how much fun it can be and showing him how exhilarating it can be to set an example about ruts and tapes and loops does not, in *all* aspects approach skydiving. (Can you get *your* mother to skydive with *you*? Now *there's* a picture!)

How universal seems to be the notion that we are stuck and fixed and in an eternal orbit based on past events. We are to a great extent the people who decide we are stuck. We decide that the name of the game is to get unstuck. And since no one has decided to even suggest otherwise, off we go to the races . . .

As for my Icelandic friend, she returned home for a vacation, taking the time to send me a card bearing a beautiful scenic photograph of her village. She later reported how, all during the trip, friends had spoken up telling her how much she had changed, how pleasant the differences were, and that they could not quite put their finger on what was going on. Some, she said, had asked for more information, and although she described our exchanges as best she could, it was, as she laughed in the telling, something of a challenge. One just has to *be* in such energy.

Some Thoughts:

1. Bringing relaxation and a refreshing outlook to the problems of others provides the same for you. It's the fastest way to ensure there's such an atmosphere for you to enjoy.

2. We often are conditioned to wait for permission outside of ourselves. Offer others permission to be more gentle with

themselves, and if they choose to take the opportunity, you have changed society.

3. Give yourself permission to keep having awesome and memorable personal interactions. These you can keep. Once you've had enough of them, it becomes easier to realize how we really are all connected, and you can share and grow accordingly.

4. There can be much struggle in the inner knowing that we don't have to struggle. Becoming solution-oriented on the outside can help bring that same approach on the inside.

5. Staying in issues keeps you there.

6. Bring laughter and a comical sense of what we do to ourselves and our society.

7. Serving Where You Are

"*Wow!*"

The eighteen-year-old could put it only that way. He had no other words for the experience except "*Awesome!*"

He'd been watching me give a public talk about my work and, he said, all of a sudden he was able to discern a blue glow around my shoulders and head—his first experience of perceiving an aura. This refers to the energy that emanates from people as they act and think. He'd been wanting to see auras for a long time, and had been wondering how on earth he should prepare himself, study for it, or reach for the ability.

All of a sudden, it was his.

But that wasn't the only reason he had wanted to come to see me.

Here was an eager young man bursting with the desire to serve others and to serve his God. He told me how he had been praying regularly to be led to service and to be a servant of God in walking his path. It seemed so hard, though—so vague, and involving so much waiting.

And why of all times and places, was he able to see the light around me?

We covered quite a bit of ground. First off, I asked him to remember the atmosphere in the room where I was speaking, and the energy that had been, if one could see it, swirling in the gathering. He remembered that we had been sharing about uplifting thoughts, inspiration for self and others, remembering to remember that oneness does not have to be a struggle, laughing at what we put ourselves through, without being demeaning to ourselves and others. And practising a bit in practical terms how we each affect the atmosphere around us.

Given that flavour very much present, did it not stand to reason that the probability of "sight" would increase? I had to point out that this young man's then unspoken intent as to why he wanted to "see" had a lot to do with it. We spoke too of the energy he had been putting out in prayer for quite some time.

We also touched on the concept of *reputation*. All energy is seen and felt by the universe. Everything we do has an impact. This means, for example, that how we pray—in joy, thanks, fear, knowingness, confidence, or doubt—is picked up. How we problem-solve, how we gossip, how we appreciate, how we inspire—it is all noticed.

This gives power and impact to our presence. Under the laws of physics it has always been true. When we become conscious of this, it becomes a responsibility, for it widens our ability to respond. Since you are "here," how are *you* and how is the young man in this story perceived by the universe?

On to his concerns about *how* and *when* and *how much practice* . . . It was a strain just listening to him. But listen to a person long enough and he will begin to give you clues. Like the nature of his summer job. It seems that this fellow had landed a rather unique position. Here's what he ended up doing . . .

Three buildings dominate Parliament Hill in Ottawa. Of the three, the East Block had been restored by the Federal Department of Public Works to reflect the atmosphere of 1872. A series of rooms were open to the public, including the former office of Canada's first prime minister, Sir John A. Macdonald.

Into this setting, the department placed actors prepared to play the role of people of the time.

And sitting right before me was the very chap chosen to play the part of that feisty Scot, Sir John.

I made a suggestion.

"I've heard of that tourist attraction, and I knew about the actors, but it's an honour to be chatting with you, Sir John!" I began. He acknowledged me with a rather fitting and practised brogue.

"Suppose," I said, "that you were to embrace your appreciation for the energy people put out and you were to just sit and know that wherever we are, we influence. With that in mind, fully appreciate how many people, in the role of tourist, pass by your presence in a day. How many individuals, from how many walks of life, from how many lands . . .

"Now, take the event of having seen my aura. Add to it your prayer about wanting to serve, and mix in what we have shared on the subject of making things too hard and too much of a struggle. Add fun. Mix in setting an example. What happens?"

"Man, I feel so *big*!"

"Sure beats *trying*!"

There's a postscript to this one.

Some time later, the same fellow came to see me again. He couldn't wait to relay how, soon after our meeting, he was approached by a teenager who was in tears. She had wandered into the room, accompanied by other visitors, where this young man was playing his part as Sir John. The actor "played the crowd," glad-handing and joking with and greeting the tourists. They moved on, including this young woman.

Now she had backtracked, leaving her companions to press forward.

"How did you do that?" she asked through her tears.

"Do what?"

She went on to explain how she had been grieving for weeks over the loss of her best friend, who had been killed in a car accident, trying to hold herself together and move on while not by any means having dealt with how she was feeling.

"You touched me on the shoulder as you were passing among us, and all of a sudden this enormous peace came over me and all my pain vanished, all my sorrow went away!"

This fine young man shared with her for a while and then the two strangers parted.

The office of Sir John has seen much history in its time, and many moving events, for it has oft been used as the site for television broadcasts by subsequent prime ministers. But perhaps one of the most unusual stories its walls can tell is the one about "Sir John" and the relieved young lady.

Some Thoughts:

1. Interaction need not be formal or rehearsed or expected in order to be profound, effective or moving.
2. Constant prayer raised to the heavens to be of service may drown out one's observation of what is being achieved.
3. Atmosphere created with intent and in a spirit of expansion rather than correction can yield up wonderful experiences.
4. Look around you. Servants of God are in the most unlikely places.
5. Keep this story in mind about what I call "the pinball effect" of human interaction—that one good turn or one deeply appreciated insight in one place can ricochet in such a way that it affects the lives of many people, some of them far-flung from your own experience. Ponder how this relates to the chapter entitled "Being There."
6. If you go up to Parliament Hill, be courteous to the man acting the part of Sir. John. It's likely that by now he's being played by another individual. The poor unsuspecting soul might have a bit of a time if you approach him and ask that he touch your shoulder . . .

8. One Doggone Ghost Story

Perhaps common sense shouldn't be called that, for sometimes it seems it isn't all that common. Bringing it along with you can be loads of fun, even in the most serious of situations, especially in cases where there seems to be little of it present. These are what I call, "*Who woulda thunk!*" moments. One of the best of times to do so is when one is called out to perform a de-haunting.

From time to time I get phone calls from people who are at their wits' end about a disturbing energy in their homes. They've called in psychics, even ministers or priests, but to no avail. Often even the uninitiated or unschooled can feel a presence. They can find themselves either groping for explanations or walking away in exasperation. I'll tell you about a time I received one of those calls, an event that packed much learning about how *common sense* helps us all.

It seems that a woman living out in the countryside had an energy in her home so disturbing that even her dogs would not enter the kitchen. Of dogs there were plenty—she was a dog obedience trainer of some renown, to the point that her training engagements sent her all over the world. And what does that show us? It's a joy to be great at what you do when what you do is of service to others. There was no doubt she had passion for her work.

Psychics and clergy had told her to move and said she had to get out of such a troubled residence, the sooner the better. The dogs were always acting up, she reported. They would not sleep and were not comfortable in the house, some of them even refusing to enter. What was she to do? I agreed to investigate.

As I walked into the home, I noticed that the kitchen was practically bare, as if someone had moved everything out in order to paint or renovate the room. All the utensils were piled in the dining room. Clearly, food preparation had been moved well out of the kitchen. Literally bringing *common sense* with my aura, I walked through the bungalow, occasionally stopping to make an energy adjustment here and there, standing still at times, or moving slowly through a space. The dogs began to stir from their various states and positions. My client stepped back, thinking it too bold of me to enter the kitchen that she and her dogs shrank from. In I walked anyway. And didn't I bump into a solid shaft of energy situated in the middle of the room.

Of course, if you bump into something, it might be wise to say, "Excuse me!" which I did. I could tell it was the energy of an older man, who I surmised was the former owner of the house. His back was bothering him so, with his permission, I proceeded to do some work on his spine. He straightened up.

My client could feel a heaviness lift from the residence. The dogs began to move about.

"The man wants to talk to you," I reported to my host. "Let's sit down in the living room and chat." My client was too busy noticing the change in behaviour of her dogs. Overriding her exclamations that a three-way discussion was too impossible to imagine, I reminded her of the outcome she had asked me to obtain in the first place, and that she could unmistakeably feel the relief already. We settled ourselves and began.

It seems the man in question was indeed the former owner, her uncle, who had died about two years previously. He was a businessman, and had some concerns about how his niece was running her operation, which he believed could be done more efficiently. As I tend to do, I negotiated a pact of teamwork between the two of them, reminding him what kinds of approaches cause people to blossom and change, and what kinds of tactics, like standing stoically in the kitchen in frustration, do not. My client continued to wonder at the dogs, telling me that certain ones (for she knew all their personalities and traits well) were now uncharacteristically calm, even sleeping.

We talked about certain things that would help out her uncle in his helping her. My client told me that deep down she had been drawn to animals in part because she has trouble dealing with people.

"Well, to let you in on a secret," I said, "people *are* quite difficult. Don't blame yourself."

She added that she had more trouble dealing with the dog owners than with the dogs.

"And this is unusual?" I told her about the veterinarians who said the same thing.

"How do I handle the owners?"

"Don't bother. Every businessperson knows that good news travels fast. Do you talk to dogs?"

"Yes."

"Does it really bother you that some people would think you're crazy for doing so? Does it bother the dogs?"

"No."

"So tell the satisfied dogs to tell other dogs about your work, and to bring their owners with them, all along pretending to the humans that it's the dogs who are being trained. Low overhead, high traffic, satisfied customers."

Relieved homeowner/pet owner/businessperson. Happy dogs. One relaxed relative. And one kitchen back in business.

Some Thoughts:

1. "I don't know" can be a cause for excitement, or a cause for fear. Make up your mind. To be sure, prudence is needed for safety, but the bringing of joy where you smell fear is to help others pass through their learned limitations.

2. Ghosts, animals and living space all constitute, move, contain and affect energy. That being the case, flow with it and appreciate how your presence can always change an atmosphere.

3. Let the woman and her dogs and her uncle enjoy having served you by saving you time and "lessons" of your own. Give thanks to them, and such an expression of thanks will show up in *your* energy. Not a bad thing to broadcast.

4. Why did the uncle stay in the house? Who cares? Why did he not "go to the light"? Who says he wasn't already there? Respect and calm actually vibrate and can be felt by many and seen by some, too. It's not important whether or not connections are there, it's about what we choose to do with them and what connections we choose to make and stand for. In this case, no one was shifted by design or "by the book," yet everything shifted for the better.

9. A Friend Comes Calling

People leave trails of energy wherever they go. Psychics know this, and some can pick up a sense of past events that have taken place in a particular location. People who have *no* knowledge of history can find themselves somehow mysteriously transformed when they happen to cross a field they didn't know was the site of a long-ago battle. Agree with it or not, this phenomenon has led police around the world to openly and professionally call upon psychics to help them solve cases. Applied with integrity and intent, such intervention has been known to turn baffling situations around and be successfully brought to a close.

The fact that we leave trails means that we certainly create or put out energy where we are. What would happen if we were to embrace this truth and apply it to create a better world?

It's a topic that came up during a phone call I received from a church minister in Tennessee. She'd heard of the work I do, and had been introduced to me by e-mail through a mutual friend.

Not wishing to thrust her life upon me, she was very apologetic about having quite a shopping list of things she wanted to check out with me. After we'd set some of them down before us, so to speak, I let on that I had—with very powerful psychic powers (read *sarcasm* here. *Please!*) come upon a classic case of *minister-itis*. She gave her permission for me to elaborate, which I did, by intoning:

Ladies and Gentlemen!

It sure is hard being a minister. Man, it drains one of energy at times! Boy, you have to balance physical world needs with congregational spiritual demands and try to have a private life and be on call all the time. You have to be seen to set an example while working on private demons and looking for answers as fast as they are posed, and boy, that inter-church politics thing with various personalities tied in with a theme of togetherness that congeals on Sunday—because that's what we're here for, but we can't necessarily spread it around during the week while having to deal with the fact that this is the only congregation for miles of this denomination.

Then there is the matter of working on raising the consciousness of these people while not being able to put your feet up . . .

Well, the reaction was as if this woman had been given a weeklong spa treatment in two minutes flat. And through words uttered by a Canadian worlds away from her charming Southern accent. Using *spirit*, no less. And embracing the very theme of connectedness and appreciation she spreads to others!

How did I "pick up" on this so quickly? It was not, I explained to her, a matter of being talented or trained—or so I had discovered. It had more to do with my intent in connecting. As is a foundation of all my work with thought and energy, we would do well to begin demonstrating how the quality of two strangers meeting can be more uplifting, more refreshing, more joyous, more outward in its outlook, and completely inspirational.

"It's not about fixing, it's about my saying, 'Thank you!' to a person whom I have never met who has been on a road serving herself and others," I explained. "It's also about demonstrating something to the surrounding energy. Compassionate behaviour teaches how the identification of 'challenges' need not leave the observer or the person subject to scrutiny any less empowered than they were before something was noticed."

That means that noticing something and, when one is given permission, acting upon it uplifts the practitioner and the person who for the moment is in the role of, shall we say, the client.

I did have her follow me in an "on behalf of" declaration, which, as I show people, lightens your load even as you face a challenge. This, she reported, immediately changed the energy around her for the better.

We continued sharing about the connections between people. Our thoughts returned to the notion of how people broadcast energies with their beliefs and thoughts. How they do this indeed at some level leaves trails.

As long as we seem to leave some kind of an energy imprint behind us, I asked her if she would be interested in using this phenomenon to continue her work as a minister *and* to make her own journey more interesting and more vibrant.

I got a yes.

I reminded her how in some societies people are raised in a tradition in which they bring food or a gift when they enter a home. It denotes giving, connection, friendship, and acknowledgement of connection. It's also about an action played out to support a conviction. It declares, "I mean what I say!"

I asked her a question: If energy is energy in *any* form, and people *do* leave energy trails, what would happen if everyone visiting any place, especially people's homes, decided to consciously leave a "gift" of energy? It could take the form of a blessing, a thanks, an acknowledgement, a declaration to help clear out what is no longer needed. Think of the possibilities!

"We'd have a *ball*!" I concluded. I expressed how I'd decided to do just that when I was around and in various locations, and to do it also in conversation.

"A good candidate for this would be your place of worship," I observed. "From time to time it's possible that there are visitors to your church. That would be a great opportunity for them to come bringing 'energy gifts' in gratitude for the prayers, the friendship, and the sense of community. People who do this kind of giving quickly get a sense of what a location is lacking, what it could use, what could refresh it. Then it becomes fun knowing that what you are bringing—a sort of energy bouquet, for example—really makes a change in the world."

I asked her to think of her place of worship, which I had never seen.

"Think of me walking in there as a total stranger, as a Canadian, as a man who is not one of your particular form of faith. Lots of potential for new energy to meet new energy. And as I walk up the aisle and stand in the middle of the building with its walls all around me, I can intone an energy gift such as this one:

Ladies and Gentlemen!

Thank you for having me here. Thank you for the provision of this place of prayer where people can meet in community and help one another. Thank you for the time taken here from the hustle and buzz of life to give thanks, to reflect, to grow and to rest.

On behalf of all pilgrims, I would like you to notice what happens to my energy and to the energy of this space as I acknowledge that I am a mere visitor here, and yet I also realize how important this role is.

Notice the corners and cracks here and there, in an energy sense, where the atmosphere is tired, perhaps stale, perhaps stagnant. Let in fresh energy. Watch what gifts gratified visitors can leave as they travel. And watch what happens to any weight on the shoulders of the residents here. This, in a way, is a clear example of displacement. Bringing in one form of energy causes other energy to melt away.

It also sets an example about the universality of us all, that a problem or a worry or an illness in one of us can vibrate in many ways that are the same in us all. Even the worry about worrying about it or the sense of being trapped or misunderstood or beyond help are as common as the air we breathe. By displacing energy, one is not robbing anyone of hard lessons or relieving anyone of responsibility. One is teaching energy and people and the atmosphere what else can be done as we walk among each other.

Thank you so much. Please go and tell others how this is done and that you have witnessed it. So goes a life of service that is at the same time light and fascinating."

I asked my caller, who had been on a path of studying energy and getting to know more about her place in it, to stop for a while and check the main hall of her church to see what she saw in her mind's eye, to feel any changes in the enclosure as a result of the prayer.

She told me how she could feel a lightness in the worship space—a lightness that, upon reflection, she now could sense had been missing. And she reported how what she discerned as a sense of spirituality had in just the short time of that declaration increased by what she guessed was somewhere around "forty-five per cent." She could also feel more space, more joy and a more relaxed atmosphere.

So it is with all of us—in taxis, in churches, in stores, on crowded highways, in lineups, at the beach, and in hospitals. Working to eradicate anything can take effort. Deciding to demonstrate what uplifts, what is fun and what brings joy is a lot easier.

Some Thoughts:

1. You are the only one who can bring original thought to where you are. That is the God-ness in you. You can decide when and where to bring uplifting energy. And you can do so in the full knowledge that you are seen and heard.

2. I sometimes quip that it is wiser to work with energy than with people. That's because people can become so complex and so bothersome and so stuck and so preoccupied and so . . . And so it goes, on and on. Working with energy, with your thoughts and your declarations and with the atmosphere really gets results. If you do so in any way that is less than uplifting, the results will come back to you. If you do so in love and inclusion and celebration, those results will come back to you as well.

3. Who taught you how to bring energy gifts to the environments where you walk? Probably no one. What's more, energy is more likely to be waiting for you to act, waiting for anyone to act, than it is ready to jump in and take things over. We often pray to be led, but are not ready to lead, and we pray for signs, knowing in some unspoken way that if we are to receive signs, there must be someone out there already who is involved in creating these markers. When we ask for signs, we know we are not alone. That being the case, work with the energy that is there. Get up and get started.

4. There's talk and then there's doing. Wanting something and having it are two different things. Like many aspects of working with energy that are included in this book, wandering into a new space and bringing enlightened and inclusive thought is an idea. Once it is practised it becomes a reality. And a new thing moves from the extraordinary to a habit and from a habit to a way of life.

5. We marvel at how some tribes, including the Australian aborigines, are able to sense where they are. They are

known to be able to find invisible "energy markers" left by others, and to create their own markers as they move across the landscape. It is not all that mystical. It has more to do with practice. Go ahead with fun, ease and joy to bring it back to yourself and to us. The next time you are a guest in someone's home or place of worship and you are being treated with respect and hospitality, give thanks. As long as we do leave energy imprints, part with having left a sense of peace and appreciation. You might say to yourself, "Watch this! I am radiating an energy of love that can be seen in the room. Thus, I teach, I set an example, and I accomplish something." After you have done this a few times, all you will have to do is know that it is done when you so much as think of the process.

10. A Busman's Holiday

I've lost count of the people who have come to me seeking a safe and respectful place in which they can talk about experiences they believe would evoke ridicule. Just as numerous are the times people ask, "*Why is this happening to me?*" or, "Am I going crazy?" or just, "*Why me?*" Their intuition is strengthening, or their ability to foresee is opening up, or perhaps they are having dreams that are more vivid, or their perceptions of beings and energies are becoming more frequent.

Just as often, I explain that it is exactly like the conundrum of "Which came first, the chicken or the egg?" The veil is coming down and we are being affected just as much as energy around us is changing. It is not "we" or "they," it is *us*, and this is the time we are living in. Like all other "ages" before us, this one has its own characteristics that, one day, will be looked back upon as a significant time in the history of humanity.

So it was with the public transit bus driver who called seeking counsel about his sensitivity to the energies around him. He wanted to know why it was that, when at the wheel, he could feel the accumulation of energy that had built up from other drivers—for city buses can often involve four, five, or even six drivers in a twenty-four-hour period.

Was he in fact weird to be able to sense the tensions and stresses of the previous occupants? While we were on the topic, he also wanted some insights as to why he seemed to be so tuned in to the moods and feelings of those dozens of people who each day passed him at the door of his bus.

My contention, I told him, is that people are becoming more and more sensitive to the long-standing power of groups and individuals to "pick up" thought. Part of the reason for this, I say, is that we have "no place to go" anymore, no place to move. We are bombarded by choices and commitments, by new radio and electromagnetic frequencies, and by options never before dreamt of by our ancestors. After all, we can not only read about or watch incidents halfway around the world instantly or within hours, we can also travel to almost any spot on earth in a matter of a day or two if we put time and effort into the attempt. Add to this the bombardment of television channels, cell phones, trickster high-flying monetary scams that have cost people their life savings, and the waste of millions if not billions of dollars on fix-it social programs. Yet in all of this we cannot escape the fact that—even as we move around the chessboard of life—we remain all connected and connected to all.

We are becoming crowded in a way that is forcing us to wake up to the facts of how life *really* operates, on both a scientific and a spiritual level. With this crowding many of us have forgotten the principles of kindness, rest, accommodation and compassion, as well as how effective these and common sense are. This is a time when we need to become aware of what we create and how we have created it.

We are waking up to the obvious. We are becoming more conscious about it. We are realizing that, for most of us, we have not been handed an operating manual. What's more, we are finding it difficult to write one even as we are being carried away by the whitewater currents of rapid interaction.

We've been affecting each other for eons at rock concerts, medieval jousting matches (not *exactly* the same thing), picnics, singalongs, hospital wards, and taxation offices (again, not *exactly* the same thing).

Once upon a time, tribes and separate enclaves of people could at least enjoy the benefits of some level of common vibration. It came in a form of worship, in familiarity of neighbourhood, perhaps in a common tradition surrounding food preparation.

Now? It's everyone for themselves. Whether more people are seeking because of an increase in discomfort—or more walls are coming down in dream states, increased intuition, a very human exhaustion from struggling, or an unseen influence that says it's time we grew—awareness is happening all around us.

Some people pray for relief from a personal conundrum. In some sense they would give *anything* to be free of an internal split or conflict. They feel misunderstood and threatened with ridicule about what they are privately struggling with. They long to have somewhere where they can share.

And so the bus driver was sitting with me.

Like so many occupations, being in it and observing it from the outside are two different things. That's why insurance brokers, firemen, choirmasters, musicians, retailers and muffler repairmen have their own worlds as much as they share common human feelings, wants and needs. I asked the bus driver to consider embracing what seemed to be a very present and very real extrasensory perception, and to use it to serve himself in the service of others.

Serving himself in the service of others.

How many bus drivers are there? How many drivers, even those who have exclusive use of their vehicles, are being consciously and subconsciously affected by that workspace, with all its confined energy, its exposure to traffic over the left shoulder and all manner of persons climbing aboard to their right? How many citizens have absolutely *no* idea what it is like to work such shifts, deal with other drivers, juggle passengers at the door—not to mention the jostling and behaviour going on over one's back shoulder? We should trade jobs for a day.

"Combine your knowingness *and* your service. It sure beats trying to turn your awareness *off* or worrying about what is happening to you," I suggested. "What would happen if you declared how your intent can clean up the residue of previous shifts? Not only that, you could:

1. Demonstrate how you are becoming aware of your abilities.
2. Settle your angst by doing something positive.
3. Set an example of how others from all walks of life in your situation can choose to act.
4. Serve your fellow drivers.
5. Be able to present a more relaxed energy to your passengers.
6. Teach by example how energy affects energy; and uplift those around you in a way that presents *no* strain to your emotions, your attention or your body.
7. Move the practice you gain in working with this situation into other aspects of your life with ease while being able to keep this technique in your toolbox forever."

This bus driver and I practised with a declaration:

Ladies and Gentlemen:

On behalf of all bus drivers, I would like to show you what happens when my own energy fully acknowledges how people leave traces of their presence. They always have and they always will. That being the case, let's do something grand with this phenomenon of physics in a way that people are served and stress is reduced. I want you to watch what happens when, upon sitting in the driver's seat, I dispel former energies so that drivers who arrive after my shift feel refreshed when they sit in this seat. I know what it would feel like if someone did this for me, and now I am demonstrating how it can be done so that others can learn.

I know all too well about the stress that can be brought on board by passengers. Once again, I would like to show how energy that presents itself in a calm and uplifting way can serve the world exactly where I am. This is how it is done. Demonstrating it is more fun than trying to do it. Feeling it accomplished is more fascinating than hoping that it works.

I would like to show you what happens to my left shoulder and left side as I begin to let my energy body—that essence coming off the body that is around each and every individual person—help me to move smoothly through traffic and to set an example with unseen aspects of myself as to how traffic can be smooth and easy. And then I'll take note of the difference in my feelings and in my body at the end of a shift. I'll be able to stack things one on top of another—better health, lighter feelings, increased circulation, greater satisfaction, self-sustained cheerfulness—and be able to show people how it works. Let's give it a try on my next shift! Thank you!

Not bad for becoming "aware" of the residue in that driver's "hot seat."

It's an old phrase in English, this term "busman's holiday." It refers to a situation in which one's recreational activity—something that perhaps one enjoys on a holiday—ends up being very similar to one's own daily and regular work. It derives from the notion that a busman could very well spend his vacation travelling on a bus, and might well have to do so in order to get to his vacation destination. It's an observation that goes back at least to the 1890s.

In a sense, we're all like that bus driver. We eat, sleep, play with, run away from, organize and seek *energy*. We influence it and are influenced by it. We work in it and play in it and even when on vacation move through it and affect it.

Most of us have been breathing for the greater part of our lives. Very few of us, if we do not have respiratory problems, give a thought to the idea that there won't be oxygen in the next breath we take. We're not *that* hyper-vigilant. So it is with much of the new awareness that can appear in our lives. Rather than being preoccupied about it, we can know that we travel in a sea of thought and energy anyway. That being the case, we can become practised and mindful about what we choose to do with it.

This fellow isn't the only bus driver to whom I've introduced those notions. As long as we have transportation systems that depend so much on these ladies *and* gentlemen who chauffeur us, providing them *and* ourselves with refreshing and workable outlooks that reduce stress and raise health *makes a lot of sense*.

This particular driver tried the techniques on for size and reported all the effects we had chatted about. What this also means is, that somewhere—somewhere close to you—there is a human being in some circumstance or occupation who is using what they know and what's coming to them for the benefit of us all. This could become catching.

Consider This:

In tribes that many of us consider to be wiser, more grounded, and more connected to nature than our own, there was and still remains a tradition called *shamanism*. Tribe members are encouraged to remember their connection to nature and to give thanks for what they have received. An admission of "sixth sense" just, well, *made sense*. Their "bus drivers"—in a manner of speaking—(referring to anyone in any corner of the group) were encouraged to embrace this connection, to apply it to their daily lives, to use it to serve. No one got stressed over it, not they, not their community, not their friends. You would not have been able to find one of them confidently making his or her way through the woods without a compass, yet homing in on his or her destination, saying, "They're going to lock me up if they ever find out I actually knew where I was going!"

If one has an intent to get somewhere, the point is to get there, with a minimum of fuss and a maximum of fun, ease and joy. What's more, people schooled, chosen and/or gifted in sensing were honoured in these groups, and continue in many cases to be. When you look around, we sure seem to be behind the times, as advanced as we believe ourselves to be.

Some Thoughts:

1. Work where you are.
2. Appreciate that awareness of energy is growing.
3. Bring joy to your influence. Use it to set an example.
4. Relax. We're *surrounded* by energy. Might as well show others how easy things can be.
5. Expand your prayers to serve others even as you yourself are served.

11. How We Heal; How We Choose to Heal

In 1886, Ticknor and Company began to serially publish tales written by Lucretia P. Hale about a bumbling and comical family. *The Peterkin Papers* relayed how the Peterkin family often got themselves in a twist over some problem or another. Like as not, they'd toddle off to the unnamed "lady from Philadelphia" for advice. And their neighbour's answers seemed so wise and simple it almost hurt to acknowledge it.

In one of the most famous crises they faced, Mrs. Peterkin accidentally put salt in her coffee, leaving her family to wonder what to do about it. They brought in the chemist, who poured in all manner of antidotes and concoctions, one after another. Since these only worsened the situation, off they went to the "herb woman," whose interventions proved just as unfruitful. Finally, Mr. Peterkin and the children go to see "the lady from Philadelphia," who promptly suggests that Mrs. Peterkin pour herself a fresh cup of coffee.

Would that life were so simple or that people worked in such a fashion! Many tribes, including our own, as Ms. Hale proves, have legends and fables that point to the wisdom of simplicity.

Sometimes the complications that arise in our lives are not as innocent, nor are they reversed so easily. That's why I tell the story of Bruce Rymer.

Canadian Bruce Rymer went public around 1991 about his real identity, in a move that took much courage and was no doubt liberating in its effect on himself and others. Born as a male twin, Bruce and his brother experienced urinary infections as infants, leading their parents to decide, based on professional advice, to have the two boys circumcised. Bruce's operation went awry, leaving him with no penis—*burned off*, in fact, in an unconventional form of circumcising—with no chance in those days for reconstruction. Authorities advised, counselled and guided the Rymers to raise Bruce as a girl. They went ahead with related reconstructive surgery.[2]

The results were disastrous, in spite of widely heralded acclamation and claims in the media of how successful the then-cloaked identity of Bruce had been. But he had balked at playing with dolls, putting on

---

[2] Bruce's story was profiled in the television program *Sex Unknown*, which was aired as part of the series *Nova* by the Public Broadcasting System (PBS) in the United States in October 2001.

makeup, wearing dresses and watching his breasts grow through artificial chemical intervention. Eventually a tomboy, an outcast and a recluse, Bruce, raised as "Brenda," came out of a very different kind of closet. He cast off this pretense—which had in fact been that of the adults around him—and acknowledged who he was.

The need to make such a decision to change his gender had in fact sprung from a literal and tragic accident that had irreparably damaged a healthy penis on a healthy boy. Bruce's mother reports how she was informed that operations and a "nurture over nature" upbringing such as Bruce's had been successfully accomplished before; but in fact the authorities involved knew it was experimental.

Bruce now lives as a man under another name in a marriage with a woman, the two of them caring for her children from a previous relationship. Reconstructive surgery has given him a penis. Bruce's story stands out as a tragic example of how we can be so quick to intervene, only to go down complex and experimental roads along which we experience arrogance supported by professional status, not common sense.

The matter wasn't about Bruce at all. Parental, professional and adult fears were running the show: fears about *potential* psychiatric problems and his adjustment and ability in the future to deal with the results of the bungled operation. Those in a position of influence would have been wiser to acknowledge the situation for what it was: the destruction of his penis by what seems to have been negligence (the use of an unconventional form of circumcision). Instead, they became enmeshed in tribal fears we have about being different. One can be the victim of a tragedy and still be well adjusted within the self—which is far more feasible perhaps than trying to change one's whole identity to fit the aftermath of a surgical accident.

Without any bitterness toward one party or another, or one faction or another, a spiritually wholesome view of the world can embrace professionals and parents and patients and those affected by mistakes, and even those who made the mistakes, but it takes leadership to foster such an environment. When no one around you is bringing such sense to the table, it may be your turn to do so.

Some Thoughts:

1. Our tribe is no different than any other in that there are ways of seeing the world that constitute what "should be."

Living with principles may not take the pain away from this life, but it sure makes things easier in the long run.

2. Dwarfism, blindness, birth defects, as well as mutilations later in life from accidents or attacks, do occur. Embracing people in these situations does not mean turning away from their situations, nor does it mean projecting onto them your expectations of how they feel because you know how you think you would feel in their shoes.

3. People in pain or who feel different or are treated as if they are very different from ourselves can put themselves into boxes as outcasts and keep themselves there until someone comes along and opens a door. Likewise, we can collectively *keep* people in boxes through pity, ostracism, expectations and widely held misconceptions.

4. Some energy is just universal, plain and simple. Compassion is one. And respect that uplifts and empowers is another. They are free and priceless.

5. We are constructed of aspects. Part of us has gender; part of us may be a taxpayer, a citizen, a hockey lover, or one who loves to cook. Balancing and harmonizing these is part of life for ourselves and for others. To conduct energy is to transmit in a very real and scientific electrical sense, and to lead and blend and create in a very musical and artistic sense. Be an influence in both.

12. Sharing the Wealth

It can be satisfying to *feel* and *see* how one's positive influence spreads and has repeated effect. It can produce a high that many of us were taught to suppress for fear that any swelling of pride in one's work might lead to a swelled head. Nonetheless, when you are connected to the *principles* of energy and you leave posturing behind, it's possible to feel the ripple of satisfaction without prejudice. It can waft over man, woman and child regardless of circumstance. Given that people tend to gravitate toward stories that inspire, it's gratifying to hear of instances in which people's lives are changed for the better in amusing, easy and joyous ways. When you're part of this, then it's truly *through* you and not *by* you that such empowering change takes place.

Consider where you place yourself. When you think of yourself principally as a healer, be prepared for disappointments, setbacks and occasions when things don't click; for this happens in interventions by medical doctors as much as it does in those by touch healers. There is an alternative: You could choose that wherever you are, you are demonstrating for a wider purpose, and indeed to a wider audience, how compassion and humility, wonder and ease do play a part. Your entire presence relaxes. You are not running the show, but are influencing it, and you always have.

Look at the topic of prayer. When one is in a position to teach how to pray, there is no better way to do it than to pray in an uplifting, inclusive and compassionate manner. The laws of physics dictate that the energy that comes off you when you are in a given state must be picked up and felt by the energies around you. You teach by doing; and you put out the feeling in order to demonstrate how it is done.

In everyday life, *show* how bringing friendship into a hospital churns stagnant energy into lively movement. Then one is embracing the universal truth that one's influence is not only felt, it can in fact be seen by some, too, in the same way that grumpiness, fear and division just as easily change a room even as we fail to immediately notice this is the case.

It's been gratifying to watch people who've been around my work in some form or another as they take it into their lives and spread its application in many forms and in many corners of life. One client told me how exciting it was to be at Mass one Sunday only to hear her priest echo many of the principles she hears around my activity. It is not *of* me, nor is it *of* this particular cleric—it is a demonstration of the universality of common sense, thinking of others, and a movement from the fixing of the world to the awakening of what we can all do. Not only am I participating, so is he, and not only are the two of us participating, we are demonstrating how thought travels and how people can choose to connect to thought that is more vibrant.

Likewise, my associate Marlyn Moffitt has applied many of the things she has practised here with some of her own training in modes of change such as *Reiki* and touch healing. This combination has had its own successes and has fostered its own stories that only further underline how sharing the wealth creates ripples of uplifting change. Among her experiences she has one to share that serves to reinforce what happens when, hand over hand, we pass along what it is like to live what the soul already knows:

> From time to time, as part of my practice, I offer customers at a beauty salon the opportunity to experience the relaxing effects of my work with energy, sometimes applying the healing tradition called *Reiki* as I do this. It was in that setting one day that a client gave me permission to place my hands on her shoulders. My sense of the enormous stress she was under was immediate, prompting me to offer a private session, to which she readily agreed.
>
> We retired to a private room on the premises, where I continued my work on her behalf. No sooner had the session with my touch healing techniques commenced, she began to cry. Thinking that I must be some sort of psychic as well who could read her mind, it was then that she declared, "You can tell, can't you. You know that I'm having an affair, don't you?"
>
> I shrugged and just listened. It was obvious that she was very distraught, and I let her continue.
>
> "Yes, I am having an affair with my boss. It's *so* exciting." She paused. "I think I really want to be with him; he's so generous and kind and we have so much fun together. My friend really likes him too, and is encouraging me to be with him."
>
> "Is he married?" I asked.
> "Yes"
> "With a family?"
> "Yes"
> "And you, are you married, and with a family too?"

"Yes, we're both married with children," she replied through her tears. "My friends keep telling me to leave my husband and I don't know what I'm going to do. I find my boyfriend so exciting and passionate."

Not knowing any of the circumstances, and only knowing full well how torn and upset she was feeling, I asked, "What is it that you *really* want? To me, this all sounds like an office flirtation with exciting afternoon getaways." I asked her to just play along with me for a few minutes to see what we could do. She agreed.

"Now," I began, "look at the energy of your boss over here and tell me what you see." I paused to give her a chance to do so in her mind's eye, and then continued.

"Okay. Now look at the energy of your husband over there," pointing in another direction, "and tell me what you see." After a pause, we moved on.

"Now look at the energy of your boss again and tell me how it would feel if you never saw him again."

She said, "I would miss the times we had but we would both be just fine."

"Now look at the energy of your husband again and tell me how you would feel if you never saw *him* again."

She started to cry again. "I would feel so guilty and so sorry. He doesn't deserve this! He is so good to me and our children, he really loves me and our family, and I really love him. *Oh my God!* I can't do this to him and the kids! I'd never forgive myself. What was I thinking about? If I left it would devastate both of us, and the kids, too. Why did I do such a thing and how am I going to make it up to him for what I have done? [long pause] How did you do that? In just a few minutes you made me realize what I was doing, as well as knowing what I'm going to do!"

Our exchange lasted thirty minutes at the most. As a result of her revelation her walk, her face, and her energy changed completely. She was relaxed. Lighter. More confident in the knowingness that she had made a decision. She felt better able to handle what was going on in her life and how she was going to handle it. As she left she hugged me and thanked me for saving her marriage and helping her to avoid all the rest that could have been involved.

Some Thoughts:
1. The absence of judgment, blame, and problem-oriented fixing that brings complicated solutions sometimes makes for quick, easy, sensible turnarounds filled with common sense.
2. When one person in a situation changes, everything changes.
3. Working with energy can be so much easier than working with people.
4. People often enjoy living through another's drama. They'll even go as far as embellishing drama, complicating drama, and evoking dramatic solutions, leaving in their trail bigger questions and deeper anguish. It need not be so complicated.

13. Play Ball!

I found myself standing on stage, addressing an audience in a university amphitheatre. The spectators occupying the seats had come to hear me and two other authors. The event promoter had recognized how our work was linked by some common themes. We were a trio of individuals who had written about uplifting and spiritually expansive topics, already published as books.

When it came my turn to speak, chatting specifically about my book *The Thunder Within* took only so much of my allotted time. I wanted to use the occasion as a springboard to *move on* to related philosophies that worked *then and there* for the audience, hopefully leaving them with insights that could transform their worlds. Their having come to the gathering in a certain state, I wanted them to go away the better for it.

I called for questions.

"What," came a query from high in the seats, "would you suggest we do about interaction in the workplace that's offensive or negative? How do we protect ourselves from it? How do *you* protect yourself from it?"

"And what, pray tell," I asked, "would be the energy around a person who is spending time and energy and focus protecting themselves? And what would be the *message*? And the effect on a space and the influence upon those around them? What would be the purpose of such a spiritually aware person? We emit frequencies *all the time*! What do you *want* to emit? What signal would *benefit* your environment while making it easier on yourself?"

I asked the audience to ponder how many people in our society in their own conscious and subconscious ways put out that they're working on protection. Granted there are some very real dangers from stalkers and rapists and the like. I don't minimize the seriousness of such threats. Keeping this conversation for the moment on purely day-to-day interaction, there could be, I suggested, a lot more joy and celebration. No one disagreed.

Rather than waiting for someone to show them how to do something, what would happen if they started showing *others* how to achieve things? ("Gee," said some of the body language and faces looking down upon me in that theatre. "Me *teach*?")

"Consider this!" I invited. "I'm going to show you what you can do with your energy body even as you stand still with your physical body. I then asked a man in the crowd to shout insults at me. He did his best, but I had to get him to give it the old college try.

The audience saw me stand peacefully and calmly. "What you see," I told them, "is my physical body at rest. But what have I been doing with my *etheric* body? More insults, please!"

Well, they couldn't come fast enough. As I was verbally pelted by my volunteer, I grabbed a "ball" out of thin air, as if to catch his insults. I then juggled it, played with it, and then bounced it until, to my suitable vocal sound effects, the bounce diminished to nothing. I then stared at the "ball" as it lay at my feet.

Thoughts are energy, and energy does travel. And it does make a difference. People have been schooled in insults, but they have not been schooled, in a formal way and at an early age, in the advantages and benefits, to themselves and others, of positive speech. (See the story called "Listen Up!")

Here though, in the moment, was a turn of perspective for those gathered that afternoon. It was about possibilities and creativity. If so many of us have been conditioned to play an offensive-defensive game of chess, who in the playroom is doing anything else?

The response that day, spoken and unspoken, was certainly that of many people declaring, "Why didn't I think of that?" It was a palpable energy. Since there were people present who I knew actively applied their extrasensory perception, I asked them to report what kind of a feeling they sensed in the room. Even people not so formally tuned-in expressed a positive shift in the room.

It was gratifying to hear, some weeks later, how people who witnessed the "follow the bouncing ball" option were using it in their lives and finding that it *worked*! There was some satisfaction in knowing and feeling that my interaction that afternoon had helped someone out in yet another corner of the world. See if you can do the same.

Some Thoughts:

1. There is more to energy than meets the eye. We are told time and time again by people with expanded visual ranges, and reminded just as often by processes such as Kirlian photography, which uses a light spectrum wider than the average camera, that energy in the form of waves and vibrations that can be seen as colours does emanate from the body. That being the case, become conscious that one's "movements," seen and unseen, have an effect. Put this into practice to bring joy to your environment and to others.

2. Put out. Feedback as to how you touched the lives of others with an uplifting suggestion will come back to you.

3. Put fun into your teaching. It's not all drudgery.

14. Stretch the Table!

Dinner that Saturday evening in Montreal was part friendship, part catching up after ten years apart, and part discussion of . . . well, energy and healing and that sort of thing. My wife and I were also regaling our Massachusetts friends with stories of our recent trip to Ireland. Besides, it was a grand opportunity to put on the Irish accent that seems to come from the roots of my genealogically half-Irish soul.

I told them a true story. It was relayed to us by one of my e-mail buddies in Ireland when we had the chance to actually meet him in Dublin.

Seems that his mother had taken over the family business when his father died. This was quite a thing for a woman in the 1930s and '40s to attempt, let alone succeed at. Determined that the state would never get its hands on her funds in any sort of death taxes, she hatched a plan. She went ahead and issued a blank cheque to the trusted general manager of her company, with the instructions that, in the event of her death, he was to rush over to the bank and withdraw all her money before the authorities knew what was happening.

The years went by. His mother had a stroke. My friend received word from relatives and rushed to the hospital, where he found the priest administering the last rites to her, surrounded by friends and relatives. They withdrew to give the grieving son time alone to reflect on his great loss.

As he sat by the body, his mother opened one eye.

"Are they gone yet?" she asked

"Glory, *Muther*! You're not dead after all!"

"Of course not, son. I made a pact with God about my money and those taxes. I can't die today! It's Sunday and the bank's closed!"

My friend began to laugh so hard that he shook as the tears came streaming down his face.

"Oops, here they come!" said his mother, closing her eye once more as the friends and relations, upon hearing the commotion, rushed in thinking my buddy was beside himself in grief, tears and all.

His mother lived for another ten years.

Stories have their way of teaching us, and so it has been since the dawn of time.

Back at the table in that Montreal restaurant, our friends expressed a deep interest in my work, they themselves having situations in their lives they knew could use some insights. They began to ask how a person could cope with old habits, unlearning strategies that don't work, deflect negativity, and so on. We were getting deeper into these matters. I, for one, had lost all awareness of my surroundings.

Suddenly I felt someone standing over me, to my right. (In the work I do, I sometimes have to be careful and clarify if the person I'm referring to has a body or not. This one did, definitely.) Sure enough a cheerful, kind-looking seventy-something lady had come up to our table. It was she who was touching me on the shoulder.

"We *so* love your Irish accent!" she said, "Where did you learn to *do* that? Are you really Irish? We began listening intently to your stories and had so much fun!"

She lingered a bit, making sure she passed her gaze to each of us. She moved on, patting me on my left shoulder blade twice, and made her way out of the restaurant with a gentleman who was quite likely her husband.

We were all taken aback for a moment.

"Sure made her day!" my wife Kathy intoned.

We *had*, after all, been discussing how energy affects energy, and how people have an influence upon the energy around them and can consciously make shifts that in turn change the atmosphere in the immediate vicinity.

"*See?*" said Kathy. "Stretch the *table!*"

What had been emanating from the four of us, after all, had been joy, laughter, friendship and uplifting conversation, even as we had been sharing in a topic that was all about how people can, if they wish, choose to make life a whole lot easier.

"I wish I had stories like that to tell!" declared one man I know who heard this tale. "I wish those kinds of things would happen to *me!*"

Ideas are the key. Time and time again, as I work with individuals and groups, I impress upon them the impact of thought. What they decide, out of the blue, to hold as an intention does have an impact.

Some people might enjoy the story that's just been shared here, and that would be the full extent of their experience with it. Others might get the idea and see the physics behind it all. Still others might say, "I would like to show the atmosphere what happens when, the next time I am in a restaurant, the energy of where I am transmits joy to those around me."

Then you will have stories just like this one to share with others. And the universe will know you're in business.

Some Thoughts:

1. Listen to more stories until you get things firmly planted in your mind: Where we are and what we bring and what we choose to concentrate on produces life and situations and more choices.

2. Even as you sit there planning and hoping and wondering, that very energy is coming off you and affecting your environment.

3. It is easier to bring what you want to a situation than to work hard at checking how you are behaving and trying to correct or compensate.

4. In the true story of the Irish woman and her son, be aware of the power of faith. The two people in this story may never be known to you, and you probably would have never otherwise known that they existed. But part of their life has now affected yours. The fact that this goes on all around us all the time now can be cause to pause and to celebrate.

5. If you want stories like this to relate to others, bring joy and you will watch and feel as others around you are uplifted, just like this older lady at the nearby table.

15. Living Like It's Never Too Late . . . And Getting There Early

The questioning from this man seemed as desperate as it was persistent. "Why don't I have *guides*? I need to know where they are. Other people have them and a psychic told me that I don't have any. What have I done wrong?"

The caller, a boarder in a private home, had picked up my book *The Thunder Within* off the coffee table in his landlord's residence. Looked like an interesting read . . .

In my healing journey, which I described in that book, I encountered the spiritual concept of guides—the phenomenon of beings in spirit of many descriptions who apparently are around to help humans, guide them (as the designation indicates), and participate in a largely passive way in the ongoing drama on Planet Earth.

People *have* guides, so the story goes. And apparently this man *didn't*. What's a fellow to do?

There are many instances of individuals leading others to "new" levels of understanding in ways that actually disempower them. We are not here just to be guided, we are here to guide as well. We are not mere puppets on strings. We have free will. This we can use to discover a life that uplifts and a way of walking through life that brings joy.

Clearly the thought of not having guides was weighing heavily on this man, a German-born gentleman now in his seventies. How had he failed? Why was he not worthy? What was blocking his connection to them? All this downward energy that had entered his thoughts with the conscious or subconscious complicity of others. What a waste of time and talent!

When he came to see me, I stood behind him as he sat in a chair and put my hands on his shoulders. I simply spoke about what I feel is a bit of something that is nothing short of spiritual stupidity—a belief that the road of existence is a steep climb, a test, a graduation, and (apparently) one that is void of joy, fun, respect, new ideas, teamwork, inspiration and calm. I spoke of how the damage that direct or implied judgments upon the self and others creates tension and how this man was actually teaching the energy around him what *doesn't* work. This, in a manner of speaking, was his current service. And although it was effective, was he having fun yet?

The ideas and input kept flowing as I spoke. I asked the energy around us to notice how close I was to this man physically at the moment and that, apparently, no harm was coming to me. "Look!" I said, "I'm right here, and I'm okay. What's holding the rest of you back? Why are you standing so far away? Can't you see that this man has been taught to believe that spirit is to teach him and has no idea you are all standing around *waiting to be taught*?"

Let's get a move on!

I was not surprised that the gentleman's body relaxed as he expressed deep relief. Here was I, sitting with a man who had seen so much of history, growing up in a household surrounded by the rise of Hitler and, as he told it, berated by a Lutheran minister of a father. Berated for simply trying to express what he saw and sensed about energy and perhaps behaving in a way that seemed to border on the heretical. At the same time he was being treated as impudent.

In fact, what was returning to the room around the two of us that afternoon was the same feeling he felt as a youngster about spirits around him, about connection and about the fact that he was supposed to teach something. With great humility and care he backed into telling me how he felt that he was a leader in some unspoken sense. Yet he felt arrogant in expressing this even to one person in a respectful environment. He spoke of how often he felt as though he was a threat to people or was perceived as a threat, and how jobs and positions would not last long because of this unseen energy around him that eventually would make things awkward. Never meaning to come across as arrogant, he learned to shut up about what he sensed and knew, but could never actually get rid of it. It was suppressed, but not resolved.

"Why did it take me so long to understand this? Look at the time I have wasted!" he said.

"Not so, really," I replied. "Look at your tribe. Look at the learning experiences your parents' generation went through. Think of how many people your age feel the way you do, secretly, deep inside, in a place they dare not speak of. Why you, a young teenager somewhere in a corner of Germany in the thirties? Well, perhaps it would be better to be a girl in New Zealand in the fifties?"

It's so common it's tragic, and it's so hidden that it's comical.

He spoke of having had some sense, some knowingness about ghosts and the departed, but not fully grasping it. He could also sense, in one particularly traumatic dressing-down he received from his father about being dangerously heretical, that his father was concerned for his son's "safety" if only at the level of social acceptance even if he came to no physical harm. This often happens when adults encounter children who are open to other senses. As for the notion that things were happening too late in the day, I added something else . . .

"I come across many individuals in spirit who slap their foreheads, roll their eyes and look skyward in exasperation after considering how they behaved and how things could have been a lot easier and a lot more fun," I told him. "'Why didn't I think of that!' they tell me. So, I consider that, some day, I too will pass over. Given the high probability of that happening, what can I do *now* to prevent myself from having to go through the same frustration? How can I 'broadcast' with energy to people in all stages of existence that the same principles hold true everywhere? What, after all is 'too late'—is it in one's fifties, nineties, or after you have departed? And is there any strength to the notion of something being too early?"

I reminded him of the work I have done with couples attempting to have babies, with babies in the womb and with newborns. All in all, it's a form of insurance, in a comical way. Better parents and births and happier teenagers and adults and increased contentment in old age and more peaceful and noble deaths help me out in my life, not to mention my own experiences in crossing over. Does reincarnation really exist? In the end, who cares? Once we get the joy and the ethics and the common sense and the wisdom and the unity right around the whole thing, will it matter?

I told this client how I had received a phone call from a pregnant woman who was concerned that her unborn child would "have issues" and that these may have something to do with her. How could she prevent a crisis? How could she know what the child might have to go through and how could she, if she was on a spiritual path, prevent things from going wrong?

I had asked her to place her free hand on her tummy. "Now," I advised, "If you were a baby in a womb and you had just listened to that and felt the vibration of that, what would you think? How would you *feel*?"

"Pretty depressed."

"Makes sense. And since the two of you are so closely connected, would it stand to reason that the impact would be immediate?"

"Yes."

"There you go. You are now spiritually operational. As a matter of fact, you were spiritually operational the very moment you spoke of issues and worry and responsibility and fear and the fact you didn't know how to do something." (See the story entitled "A Busman's Holiday.") "What would happen if you declared,

Ladies and Gentlemen!

On behalf of all mothers carrying babies, I would like to show energy how I have decided that as a woman and a citizen and as a mother and a parent and as a spouse and as a taxpayer I am sick and tired of struggle. What better way to show you that I mean it than to embrace a more calm and uplifting energy in interacting with a new life. Watch this!"

She reported quick and deep relaxation. She reported less stress in her back and abdomen. She reported a sense of connection with her baby she had not felt before. Given that her native society was no stranger to the concept of reincarnation, she could see now how this was in fact something that was serving her as well, for through this, parents could become better informed about how life functions and that she, on a future arrival, would be the beneficiary of this uplifting approach. Where better to begin stopping *stopping* doing things than right here?

Having heard that experience, the German gentleman could see how all interventions can create hope and life.

I asked the gentleman to openly declare his satisfaction at rejoining his greatness when and where he is as an encouragement to others, and to spread the word with his obviously large aura, using it consciously for the first time to teach. Taking a page out of his book of experiences with the deceased, he too would eventually be "in other places." In the future, he will be able to look back on the very experience that afternoon as a victory and a celebration.

"They're standing up and cheering, these people I can now see around me!" he declared. "I don't have one guide, there is a throng in the vicinity and they have come closer!"

Some Thoughts:

1. Mentioning to people about guides, beings, angels and the like may be fine in itself, but the principles and the themes and the direction you bring with your communication can be just as significant, if not more so.

2. Speaking of yourself as a teacher and *knowing* that you are can be two separate experiences. The living of it is the message, more so than the claim.

3. Thoughts such as, "It's too late, I'm too old, too set in my ways, too unschooled, not accredited enough, too unpractised, too unprepared," and the like set the stage for what is happening. Let energy be uplifted and surprised by your refreshing approach that loves yourself and those around you with equal depth and conviction.

16. The Visit

Just how connected *are* we, anyway?

We could spend time trying to find out. We could try to *prove* we're connected. On the other hand, we could live in a way that we *know* that we're all connected, and walk through life simply *accepting* that fact. We'd become relaxed, free from a state of *trying* to prove it. Such a state of relaxation lets wondrous things happen.

Sometimes I tell the following story to illustrate this point:

Not long after my book *The Thunder Within* was published, I received a call from a man who wanted to let me know what reading it had meant to him. George, as I'll call him, had retired from work in the Ottawa high-tech sector. He went on to tell me how he and his wife had at one time visited his best friend, who was terminally ill. George told me that his buddy had announced that if there was *any* way one could connect "from the other side," he would attempt to do so and get in touch.

Some time after his friend passed away, George began to experience twitches and itching that specifically affected his nose. This happened off and on for some time. Eventually, he had a chance meeting with a woman who turned out to be somewhat psychic. It was she, to his amazement, who spontaneously explained what the twitching nose was all about. Without George even broaching the subject, she told him it was his friend doing the best he could to get his attention and make contact. Would George please, she had advised, begin to pay attention to when and where the twitchy itch occurred?

Not long after, George experienced the telltale twitching while browsing through a bookstore. *This* time he was more aware of its meaning, and he *did* stop in his tracks. But he couldn't figure out yet *why* it was happening then and there. Frustrated, he looked about. His eye caught a copy of my book, and his gaze fixed on the cover. He explained how he was drawn to the book as if directed to it. He was *sure* he was being strongly advised by his friend in spirit to read it, and he reported hearing an inner voice telling him to do so. He took the hint, and soon its pages were confirming how appropriate my book turned out to be.

But this was *not* the only reason for his call.

Inspired by what he had read, and perhaps now given the courage to speak out about mysterious happenings, George said he had a real desire that I connect with another friend of his named Bill Parfrey. Apparently they'd met at a conference held by an international organization to which they both belonged. It seems that Bill, an Irishman by then nearing seventy, had been a healer for much of his life, and was no stranger to uncommon experiences with energy of the sort I had mentioned in my writing. George thought it would be great if Bill and I could exchange experiences and enjoy the camaraderie there would be in finding a "buddy" who had our kind of energy work in common. Bill (whom people refer to as "the Parf") was sent a copy of my book. E-mails and phone calls followed. Bill was in the process of putting down his experiences on paper, and soon shared with me a draft manuscript of his biography.

The use of energy by a stranger had healed Bill of the damage he'd sustained after having been hit by a truck as a youngster. Subsequent to the miraculous intervention, he seemed to have had direct contact with knowingness and guidance, which, over the decades, led him to situations where he was called upon to heal others. Some of his stories are astounding.

The subject of this Irishman and his work came up in the discussion groups I hold regularly about energy and how it functions. Here, after all, was a man in a different land, of a different age, raised in a culture somewhat different than mine. And, for better or worse, he was a person who, for the most part, had travelled alone in this work. Yet *we* in my group, circled together as we were, had the advantage of mutual respect, helping each other out, and growing together with our questions and experiences.

As many of us tended to do by then, people checked out Bill's energy as I spoke of him. One among us was able to identify the particular form Bill's energy healing often takes as he is led to perform in appropriate ways with clients. People in the room spoke of what they got off a photograph of Bill that a good friend of his had sent me. A sense of satisfaction and a feeling of connection filled the room. We *knew* he was present and we *knew* we were sending him support and we *knew*, because he is who he is, that he was feeling how his life's work was taking on an additional facet as an inspiration to younger people.

Two years passed.

Circumstances made it possible for my wife and me to realize a long-standing dream. We visited London and then made our way to Ireland. We did not head down to Cork where Bill lived, but we spoke on the phone. Bill had been suffering from certain conditions and ailments for some time, and asked that my gang and I pray for him. With his permission I did some healing work on him as well.

Our relationship deepened in another way when I got home.

One evening, while five of us were sitting in a discussion group, I spoke of the contact I'd enjoyed with Bill while in Ireland. Not surprisingly, we could all feel Parf's energy fill the room. There was joy, excitement and satisfaction in his energy, and some relief. This was not the first time I had been told or had been aware of the man's desire to share his knowledge, to pass on his experiences to conscientious and integrity-filled people who wanted to heal themselves and others. And his energy was both surprised and filled with hope at the feeling and experience that groups such as the one we were in were possible and were forming. He seemed eager to help and to participate.

Simultaneously, those of us present could feel an emphasis on how important it is to connect, to support and to acknowledge what it is people are able to do, not in mysticism and knowledge wrapped up in exclusivity and secretive practice, but simply in kindness and creativity. As for the creativity, it was declared in the group how Parf could, as he wished during the coming weeks, lend a hand to anyone he felt he wanted to, and to be available for the respectful request for help that might come from any one of us. The room was filled with peace, excitement, gratitude and a knowledge that everyone present, in whatever form, was helping everyone else.

Some Thoughts:

1. Being aware of energy can be a lonely experience, no matter how "advanced," "holy," or "in service" a soul may be. The struggle is reflected in the lives and writings of Mother Teresa, Edgar Cayce, Abraham Lincoln, Jesus Christ, and perhaps in your life and most likely in the lives of many around you. Sages and gurus are sometimes heard to speak of life as being a never-ending struggle, infused by the need to overcome. If that's the case, why not give yourself a break once in a while? Why not demonstrate that ease can be part of it, too?

2. How do you find companionship and integrity-filled understanding for things that seem off the wall? Extend such understanding to someone else. Provide it for someone who needs it. Rather than standing around waiting for it to happen to you, create it where you are while you serve the world at the same time. It sure is efficient.

3. Never heard of Bill Parfry before? He's probably never heard of you, either! You've been living a full life all along, and so has it been for him. Instead of waiting to hear about kind people who do wondrous things to help others, *become* one of those, even if no one finds out about *you*. Many wonderful and giving people seek no notoriety, and Bill is

one of these. As he is fond of saying, "We all work for the same boss anyway." We're all connected with each other and all connected to God.

4. Move your consciousness with a touch of awareness and *intent*. It will be refreshing. Our ability to think operates much like a television antenna. Declare, "I did not know of Bill. This probably means I do not yet know of Frank, Suzette or Carlina. But I do *know*, and I now know that I know, that these kinds of people exist. And I give thanks for it."

5. Connections that function successfully are about common sense, common decency, what works, and what's acceptable in a cosmically universal way. Just being decent to people produces ripples that bring back immense returns.

6. Since we're all connected, celebrate it. And be ready to inspire others to do the same.

7. Thought is energy. Energy is part of what thought is. So, in thinking about someone, one is actually activating electrical patterns. Remember this. And use it to inspire.

17. Lost in the Woods

A client came to me wanting to explore some sort of internal split he said he had felt ever since he was a small boy. It began, he said, with what he called a near-death experience. This had been no dream, apparently; it had taken place in the middle of a forest.

The two of us explored the event.

My visitor recalled that when he was a small boy he went hunting with his father, whom he felt had cajoled him into participating. Whether the father's expectation was real or misread, the youngster felt he was there to please his father in a way and in a place he secretly did not like.

It transpired that day that the boy got separated from the hunting party. Whether he was far from them or actually close by, the sense of being lost hit him hard. He told me about the fear that had overcome him, and how he had gone through an out-of-body experience, feeling himself pulled from his mortal coil, half feeling that out of fear he was attempting to flee his predicament and half feeling he was being pulled back into the light by some other force.

He reported "coming to" after an indeterminate time lapse. After wandering and yelling for some time, he was finally discovered by the men. I did not get the impression that the reunion in any way alleviated the boy's fear, however attentive his companions might have been. Even if "being lost" or "being forgotten" had been his *own* interpretation of his world at that time, there was no doubt that the event had left an indelible mark. It makes no headway to conclude to him or in silence that he had simply been hallucinating. Who is so arrogant as to assume that the transformation had not actually taken place?

Fact is, here was a gentleman in his forties who had been split between wanting to return "home" and wanting to stay "here" ever since the age of six, caught in a conundrum he could not find anyone to talk to about in a space of respect, safety and solutions. That's a lot of split energy, something tough to carry, and a loss of opportunity and energy for himself and those around him.

So we discussed options. Away went the notions of fear-based recovery, working through trauma, overcoming memories, finding out why it happened, and the like. We chatted about near-death experiences, how tough many people find it being here, how many people actually pray, practise and meditate *for years* hoping against hope that they will have spiritual experiences akin to what happened to him.

He also conceded that other people might in fact be just as isolated and feel just as split about things they long to talk about, but for some social and other reasons find they cannot.

"What would happen," I asked, "if you embraced the experience and declared to the surrounding energy that you really do believe in the coming improvement in society, "as above, so below"? And what if the event was nothing more, but nothing less, than an attempt by energy or energies to reach you to get things started? A small boy in the woods? Stranger things have happened. Why you? Why not? Why these years of torment? No one was around to coach you! And what do we produce from this? Another available, compassionate coach for other people so they learn faster, suffer less, serve longer and are slower to gravitate to fear!

People can be very quick to weave even more issues and problems into the challenges they hear of or experience. Daring to suggest that interpretation and strategy can shine a light of even greater benefit for society can take some courage. Prayer that gives hope as much as it seeks can heal *and* inspire. Declaring one's directorship as much as seeking direction can teach as well as intervene. Creating inspiration as much as waiting for it can encourage as much as it works a muscle and strengthens an ability. Embracing one's capacity for fear and hurt *because* one is human as much as one forgives the self and others shows balance as much as it shows compassion. All this changes the energy of a body, the energy of a room, and the energy of a relationship while being uplifting and empowering.

Some Thoughts:
1. Mystical things *do* happen to people. These events are not always connected to trauma, although if they are unexplained they may cause trauma.
2. When working with people, it is important to remember how numerous the points of view can be, as well as the interpretations and missed cues that can arise in interactions.
3. It is very enabling to instantly empower people. This does not always have to involve overcoming things. At times it's even *more* powerful to remind people that, since we are all connected, what they do to help themselves actually helps us *all* to move forward more positively and more quickly.
4. Not all "work" is accomplished in one encounter, one relationship, or one process. We are fluid even in our state of being stuck. When we are civil and uplifting in more and more of our encounters there will be less and less strife. Understanding this and living this make a great difference.

18. The 20–80/60–40/90–10 Rule

It was a phone call from England this time. A message on my answering machine had notified me that the sister of a friend's girlfriend needed help. (Got it? Good thing we're all connected!) Seems she was suffering from debilitating fatigue and a throat problem that wouldn't go away. She had been sent my book, *The Thunder Within*, and after getting only partway through its pages, had hoped I could do something for her condition. It was she on the line.

My wife and I had just returned from England. In fact, we had not been an unreasonable travel distance from where she lives. Since she had been introduced to me and my work through my book, it took no time for us to get right into the concept of sharing and how that works. I gently put her through her paces. I underlined the power there is in a declaration. I described *why* one makes a declaration and how much more healing it is to include positive intent for others in our declarations as we travel through our challenges.

The woman reported instantly that she felt relaxation overtake her. Apparently she hadn't felt this way in months! Phones are wonderful things, aren't they?

"Now settle yourself and go inside," I advised her. "I want you to connect with who you really are and to get used to asking your soul from time to time about what it thinks and feels. We live in a soup of energy—telecommunications, news reports, gossip, group thought, taxes, vacuum cleaner salesmen, etc. One is bound to be connected with it. It's not a question of how you are connected, but how you *choose* to be connected, since you're going to be connected anyway."

I told her how I'd stumbled across an intuitive question that is beginning to relieve people in their personal struggles.

"Suppose," I said, "that a certain amount of what's going on in your body is the result of what is going on *around* you. Now, if some or most of what you are feeling has something to do with external influences, how much of it has to do with internal illness, unbalance and dis-ease? At the same time, as your sensitivity to energy is opening up, as your awareness is opening up, how much of the change in your body has to do with such expanded awareness, and about exposure to energies around you rather than with 'illness' *per se*"?

She settled herself, fell silent, and checked. Then she said, "I'm getting 90–10; ninety percent being how much of it has to do with energy, ten percent being related to illness conditions."

"So, if there has been trouble diagnosing your condition and creating healing, as you reported, how effective have you been as you wander here, go there, do this and that if you are addressing only the 'illness'?"

"Not very high."

My caller admitted spontaneously that she was aware of some personal ability in her to do things with energy. That feeling is more common than people let on. But just as often what we have is the drive to be a healer, with only notions and wishes and dreams. Actions and processes can become very vague and often are not manifested. The whole thing can be a tough subject to grasp—wanting to go, wanting to get on with it, having a sense of mission, and yet not knowing where to begin!

Not very enjoyable. And not very tangible. Not too productive. Boring and uncomfortable, frustrating and without any sense of having arrived. Doesn't look or feel too healing at all. Poop.

She was laughing as I expressed this, and so was I.

I asked her if there were any groups in her area such as the ones that convene in my work to share energy experiences, joy, easier ways out of pits, and strengthened senses of community.

Nope.

"Start one."

"But how?"

"And I did what?" referring to my own adventures chronicled in *The Thunder Within*. "And my credentials are what?" I asked. Did Jesus say, "Mmmm, where's my group? Who will teach me?" What about a discussion and sharing group in England, I suggested. The very kind that she always wanted to find for herself? Of all places! Who woulda *thunk*!

According to my caller, the energy around her was apparently starting to move and become even more calm. Yet, she reported, it was vibrating at a new level of excitement and anticipation. She told me how this was a great change from what she was used to feeling in her house.

Time and time again, when people come to me with illnesses who also spontaneously confess sensitivities to energy, I ask that they settle themselves for an experience of what I've come to call the *20–80/60–40/90–10 Rule*. And people do get an answer. To be sure, I fully acknowledge that experiences such as sprained ankles, broken bones, gallstones and cancer do occur. These of course ought to be looked at professionally, with care and responsibility. Even in these cases, people who find themselves in the eye of a healing process can use this rule of thumb to help themselves place even more of their attention and effort appropriately to help them bring themselves back to health.

Some Thoughts:

1. Once again, seeking something and having it are two different things. A negative feeling about being alone can best be addressed by declaring that you're fully aware you don't travel solo through the universe. Believe it. And then walk it. By using your circumstances to inspire, you can move forward with greater ease.

2. We are all affected by the social and interactive energy around us. This makes us part of the many dramas that unfold in our lives. Sometimes, what we term as negative energy is simply energy or thought caught in a rut. This applies to people, and atmospheric energy within buildings, neighbourhoods, and companies. When we dare to bring refreshing ideas and acknowledge that ruts happen, we proceed to move from *worry* about that, and move into action that is the lightness we sure wish *someone* would bring to us!

3. Put *yourself* in the picture! The international television Cable News Network (CNN) can't be everywhere *all* the time (although at times it seems like it). Like it or not, not all good deeds and successes and graduations will be caught

on tape *in the physical sense*. But they sure *are* recorded in energy. How else do you think it is that you get the feeling! The *feeling*! If it seems difficult to make a change, it probably is. Not the change. Just the difficulty. Get to know the difference. You are a living, breathing conductor of energy.

An Exercise:

You've just read a certain story in this book. Take the time to settle yourself. Close your eyes, take a deep breath, and get a sense of what has happened as a result of this information being shared, being expressed, coming off the pages, and being taken in, in some corner of the globe.

Go ahead. Stop and check. Notice and sense. Then read on.

After you've had time to reflect, answer these questions:

1. What's the sense around you?

2. What's your feeling about the exchange of information between you and these pages?

3. Do you get a sense of how the nature of the energy around us—its characteristics of respect, hope, humour, joy, lightness purpose, appreciation—affects you and others?

4. What is new for you about stopping to check the energy around you and what is being achieved by a certain event and happening like reading this chapter?

5. How has this made you more conscious of the presence of vibration?

With such increased awareness, one becomes elevated in a sense. A person is more mindful of actions and reactions and how it is that we can walk in life so that we all benefit.

19. The Nurse

She was the sister of a client from a town in a land I have never visited. There she sat, intrigued, somewhat uncomfortable, yet fascinated about what she had heard. The two of us were together with her sister and another friend. We had just finished exchanging pleasantries.

"What can I do for you?" I asked.

"I don't know," came the response.

"What occupies your time? What kind of work do you do?" I explained that since she had come to visit with the intention of going away with a benefit and since the chances of her ever being back here were slim, I thought it best that we get down to business.

"I'm a nurse." That was all it took. Her response prompted two very personal concerns that she would like to have addressed.

It seems that only recently she had asked for and obtained a transfer from her work in the intensive care unit to a staff position in the maternity ward—opposite ends of the pole of life, if you ask me.

"I couldn't stand it in intensive care!" she declared, confirming that her repulsion had caused her to judge her role as a nurse while at the same time feeling how much better it felt in the maternity ward.

I asked her whether, when she was working in intensive care, there had been practices that, deep down inside, she had felt were not appropriate, had not worked, had not been uplifting, or had not been healing. She answered in the affirmative.

I commented that even though she had felt this, our society was not totally ready to embrace the idea that we can openly talk to people in comas, and readily transform the grief and fear that understandably might befall the attending family.

She agreed that any place, including an intensive care unit (if not *especially* an intensive care unit), devoid of hope, uplifting energy, comfort, inspiration, or acknowledgement of how we are far more than our physical bodies, would be a pretty dismal environment.

As for the second concern, we talked about her strong desire to bring spirituality and energy work into the hospital—something she hesitated to do for the time being for fear of ridicule. She was also worried that there would be no kindred souls to talk to and to share with.

She feared that, in the end, the administration would probably have none of it, even if word got back to them only indirectly.

Since she was from another country, I took the opportunity to remind her how grand an idea it was that a gathering in my home, and the work already being done with groups here, could now have such an impact where *she* would be working. It was time to stop and appreciate how this kind of thinking was spreading as people helped other people.

She had been told that, using intent, I also move energy with my hands. She agreed to sit in front of me, with her back to me, as I demonstrated the ease and beauty there is in bringing exactly the energy you would wish to find around you, rather than waiting for it to happen.

With quick brushes and flicks, I worked around her. She reported greater peace and a feeling of ease.

Then it was time to move to another experience. As she was at that point sitting directly in front of a woman who was on the couch, I asked, with our friend's permission, that the nurse play the role of the nurse and our companion (bless her heart) play the role of the comatose intensive care patient. Guiding the nurse to declare an uplifting intention, I had her direct an outward palm toward her "patient."

All four of us in the room could feel the changes in the atmosphere as we talked about inclusion, healing, and joy; how curiosity can lead to both healing and discovery; and how this would help change all other intensive care units.

Again, the question of how I did this came up. And again I underlined how energy follows intent, and how bringing what you would like to see happen is easier than waiting for it to show up.

The nurse felt her fear and heaviness and repulsion surrounding intensive care work depart. Her "subject" reported joy, warmth, and healing energy.

We now addressed the notion of the maternity ward.

"Being where you are is not as important as working where you are for the majority of situations. Now that you have 'done' this for an intensive care ward, how about seeing what you can do when you go home and work in the maternity ward?"

She stood up and was given the room to pace in, to gesture, and to throw out her voice:

Ladies and Gentlemen:

On behalf of all nurses who would like to incorporate "energy work" in hospitals but think that people aren't ready for it yet, watch this! I wish to work with fun, ease and joy in demonstrating through energy and not at people how uplifting thought can be. As I make my rounds in my ward, I will talk to the infants silently as if they were full-grown adults, with respect and encouragement. I will give them the feeling of what it is like to be in the presence of an uplifted adult, an open yet responsible adult, and a person whose very presence can give them hope for their own futures. Over time, I will notice how this alleviates stress that, until now, has led to illness, and how as we show how these infants are awash in positive vibrations, they can spread this with their lives. Even now I am feeling myself more whole as the split I had inside about hiding my energy work or "coming out of the closet" is settled with no struggle for anyone, especially me!

By no means a psychic, the nurse reported the openness and the joy and the hope that emanated throughout the ward that, though a figment in my imagination, was a very real place in her world. She reported back to me by e-mail once she had returned how she had shared these experiences with nurses she knew would be both receptive and fascinated by the news of what she had experienced. And how, pray tell, was she to sustain this attitude, this energy, this uplifting view? ("I'm so far away from you!") Just think back on the meeting, I suggested, and draw from it. It is not about the danger of losing the feeling—it's about the joy of bringing it to a new place far, far away.

Some Thoughts:

1. Bring what you desire, rather than hoping you'll find it.

2. Know your presence matters, whatever your station in life.

3. Give energy around you a chance to come alive. God knows much of it could use vigour and hope.

4. Move away from trying to educate or re-educate or open up closed people; fighting the system; or assuming that the

people around you are write-offs in working with all our senses. Chances are they're waiting to meet the very person you were hoping to meet to teach you. And let energy do the talking. It saves you from being occupied with positioning and timing.

5. If it can happen in an intensive care unit, where else can it happen?

20. It's All Been Done Before (Again)

Samuel Pepys and his companions were having a particularly difficult time keeping their composure on one particular occasion. It was recorded for all time in his journal. Back in the 1600s, this English diarist happened to be in the wrong place at the wrong time, close by when the king of all the realm, the Sovereign Majesty of England . . .

Well, the king farted.

Perhaps an uncommon occurrence for a non-commoner, but it's the kind of entry that sells diaries, after all. (Mental note to me: I must watch more closely what I write about, and watch even *more* closely for things *to* write *about*.)

And what does the king's flatulence have to do with energy and healing and the advancement of society?

It's to make a point.

Some things never change.

It's all been done before.

Again.

This could use some repeating. The next time you find yourself in a kafuffle over a relationship, a scorched cooking pot, an early and already departed bus (or a late pair of feet to go with it), stop and think about what has been recorded in the diaries of humans long past. A broken heart in ancient Rome was probably just as broken as it gets. Worry over the wrath of the gods probably has not changed that much, either.

Then there's the diary written during the heyday of ancient Egypt that puts life in perspective very well. A high official writing his thoughts of the day tells of invading armies from the south, food rotting in the warehouses, and his concern for his son who has gone off to the wars. If looking at ancient Egypt doesn't make the point, then we can decipher the Latin graffiti on the walls of the Roman city of Pompeii and pick up the gossip, the scandal, the elections, and the disputes.

We feel for the Egyptian father. We feel him. We *are* him. And we've "been there, done that."

What *have* been all too uncommon are the instances of something *new* that helps us all.

The fastest way to the easiest way is to appreciate that, in the end, we are probably dealing with aspects of life that have been around for a long, long time. Daring to do something new is usually not about an entirely original thing, but, more often than not, simply putting a slightly different twist on the same old, same old.

Something that could really help us out here at the moment is a lint roller.

When I look at situations, I occasionally picture the effect of a lint roller. That's the roll of peel-able sticky paper used to remove hairs and other particles from clothes, cushions, curtains, and the like. Notice how covered the surface becomes in a short while, and how the particles that are picked up gradually reduce the effectiveness of the sticky paper, until it's time to peel off another layer, exposing an entirely new surface with which to work.

Sometimes, when I am called upon to practise touch healing on an individual, that is the image I hold in my mind as my hand approaches her body or his energy. It's as if to say,

> "Here before me stands a person of 'god-ness' who, by a variety of adventures and misadventures, has gone through doorways of various descriptions, gathering certain beliefs and experiences, and has come finally to this place here and now.

"On behalf of all energies seen and unseen, and on behalf of all human interaction that could use lighter, more cheerful, more purposeful and more enabling interaction, watch what happens when the clogged and worn energy is peeled away at a rate the body can handle in order to give life a chance to flow once again.

"There is no judgment on what has been placed there, only fascination over what we do to ourselves and to each other. At the same time, there is a real knowing that the quality of what is going on here is teaching all energy how it is possible for two people to meet at a deep level that transcends all differences. This very interaction is healing the world."

People and atmospheres don't seem to mind it when they are given a chance to take a breath, to perhaps laugh introspectively, and to become fascinated with what we do as individual and group creations and creators. The familiarity of it all is what makes comedy laughable, and reflections of ourselves, such as those found in the works of William Shakespeare, so familiar and so natural.

Given that, at some level, it has all been done before, dare to make a difference as you say, "As long as these things go on, I would like to make a difference by being more kind to myself, more open to ease, and more present. I don't want to *get there*, I want to show how it is done."

Some Thoughts:

1. Since we can look back on the lives of other people, what will be the reaction when our own life is looked back upon by others? You are at this very moment in the same position as that seventeenth-century Parisian baker, that medieval doctor, that Aztec priest, that actress in Moscow during the Second World War. And so it goes. What we can bring that is new is a peace and ease that so many of those who have gone before us fought for, searched for, and hoped for but did not necessarily experience.

2. Laugh a bit at your tribe. There are so many practices we look upon from days gone by that we find restricted, narrow-minded, lacking in insight or devoid of common sense. To us,

it looks like groups of people were stuck, or closed, or trying too hard. Consider becoming the person you would like to have had the chance to look upon as an example from the past as a good role model. And be that model for someone in the future. You will be serving yourself and others at the same time, with no duplication in effort.

21. The Eyes Have It!

Sitting before me was a somewhat exasperated woman who is known for her deep caring, her study of spirituality in her personal work and with others, her services as a social worker.

She was in a spiritual muddle-fuddle that I observe all too often among souls who have decided to take a spiritual path, not really understanding that, everything being energy, all thought and action constitutes spirituality. Spirituality becomes "something else" and is placed in its own separate box. (The joke's on us.)

It seems that this woman was, in a matter of hours, scheduled to undergo eye surgery. She was deeply troubled by the fact that, as a "spiritual" person, and all her efforts to cleanse herself, heal her woundedness, look at her dark side and walk in the light, there was no reason in the world that this should have happened. The mere fact of the operation was a sign of some deep personal failure.

Well, if spiritual paths are of such a nature, it sure doesn't make the trip attractive.

Here, I said, we have a struggling soul who is beginning to understand how energy functions. What would happen if a person were to embrace energy *as well as* the fact that we know that all states of being have an effect? How many people, I asked her, have eye operations?

"Quite a few," came the answer.

"And if you served them, what would happen? What would happen if you not only set an example, but you became one of the few people around who actually invoked fun, ease, joy, teamwork, uplifting practices, new ideas and easier healing in an operating room?"

She began to get excited.

I reminded her of how we talked, we "spiritual" people, of angels and energy and spirit, even of ghosts and people on different planes. But why don't we ask for help and suggest new plans and use these resources and demonstrate oneness? Mmm? If it can't take place in an operating room, where can it take place? And if it *can* take place in an operating room, where *else* can it take place?

I asked her to make a declaration about how this operation was to be made easier. I reminded her how this would demonstrate ease, compassion and creativity to the atmosphere around her as well as to elements and participants of which we are not necessarily aware. Many pray to saints but would swear there is no life after death. Go figure. Now she had a chance not just to seek and prepare and hope but to actually *do* something instead of constantly waiting at the starting gate.

I do know of a number of "energy workers" who have been taught to teach how physical conditions must be a reflection of negative thought. They jump into *each* new case as a problem. They see happenings as manifestations created in order to learn. And boy, do they believe learning has to be the *hard* way.

Having personally been put through that grinder on my journey with cerebral palsy and other neurological conditions, I had eventually noticed that it had not worked, and that very little healing had resulted. Uplifting, positive, inclusive and participatory intervention had done the trick.

Sometimes, to those who cart around an interpretation of judgment and darkness and blame and issues, I ask a question.

What, I say, would be your reaction to a room full of crippled spastic children of the former Soviet Union lying in their feces in cribs that had not been cleaned for months in an atmosphere of crying and lack of stimulation to the point of mental distraction and damage? Would you bring what you say are your healing abilities to heal them, or would you stand at the doorway and pronounce that these souls had created this for a reason and obviously had something they were going to have to learn? One is compassion, a readiness to learn new things, a sense of hope and a passion for discovery of how to do something and make it even better.

The latter is an over-rationalized response proving once again that every **"Why?"** gets a **"Because!"** It is the same stupid denial of solution-oriented thinking that led medicine in the 1800s, for example, to chalk up so many female experiences and beliefs to be the result of "female hysteria" for which one could be locked up.

We set things in motion that morning for the upcoming operation, this client and I. It was then a matter of waiting.

In fact, I didn't hear from her again for some time. When I did, the results were nothing short of exhilarating! What she had not told me was that, in fact, each eye was slated for surgery, and on different dates. Her operations were followed by a time of busyness and travel. This meant I would have to wait to hear from her.

She started with the news of the second operation. Apparently the surgeon who had done the first eye was not available for the following session. When she arrived for her consultation with the second surgeon, she was greeted with obvious enthusiasm and eagerness by this doctor, who asked her if she could "do it again" and repeat the procedure she had used when operated on the first time. You know, about the energy and the angels and stuff. He had greeted her, in fact, as "The Angel Lady."

Sure enough, she had really taken to heart what we had done during the session in preparing energy. She talked out loud in declarations as to how we wished for the sake of all who have operations that this should go smoothly. She spoke of her experience as a service to others and how it would set an example and show the surgeon an even better way to do things. She declared how it would cause the energy and those gathered in the room to celebrate teamwork and . . .

Apparently the operation had gone so well and the healing time of the recovery had been so unexpectedly and uncommonly quick that the first surgeon felt compelled to tell her. He also confessed that, for some unexpected reason, he had found his hands moving in unfamiliar ways, somehow doing the operation in a new fashion. This broke the dam. My client could no longer hold it in about the declarations she had made and the turnabout in her approach.

Well, as we found out, the surgeon in question could himself not keep the news in, and began reporting it to his colleagues, in direct contravention of course of the widely held belief that doctors aren't spiritual, doctors don't believe in angels, patients and doctors cannot share energy work or spiritual experiences, and both parties can be diagnosed as having a fantasy disorder.

But the second surgeon had wanted to participate! The second operation proceeded just fine.

I have discovered that hundreds of people have a little ditty going on in their heads. It's something that is having a profound effect on how fast—or how slowly—we are awakening to *common sense* and *common decency* and what works and what brings joy. It has to do with what we *expect* people are ready for, what we are prepared to acknowledge that they already realize and what is already happening to them in their dreaming, sensing, intuition or knowing. It goes something like this. You may join in:

The Limits of Spiritual Awareness
(As chanted by far too many of us)

Priests won't, cops don't
Old folks can't, children sha'n't
Patients never, bosses couldn't
Doctors mustn't, nuns wouldn't
Men wouldn't be caught, and street folk wouldn't 've thought
My spouse wouldn't dare, my shrink don't care
And I don't seem to fit.
No one understands me, so what's the sense of it?
What's the answer if you please?
I for one am *all* of these!
And even *those* souls *know* it!
Join me as we stand around
Both nature and our beings confound
Hoping someone comes along
With strength and guts to show it!
(Signed, Still Waiting)

One more chalked up for the greatness of oneness and creativity in a certain operating room somewhere in our society. What joy! And of course, some of us still think that the miracle here was about the two surgeons! Will you wait for another story, or do you dare begin creating your own influences that will bring someone else strength, inspiration and a relaxed sense of accomplishment even as you feel it yourself?

Some Thoughts:

1. When you speak to energy, declare how your intent also serves others. It has been demonstrated that prayer and declaration that also helps others while helping you has a stronger energy and a wider reach.

2. Considering yourself to be spiritual also means being kind to yourself. It means you understand that all being energy, all has a spiritual component to it.

3. While many people would privately admit that they believe in the existence of energies and people on other planes—that is, in other states of existence—they rarely invoke that truth. Know that you are not alone and that God in His wisdom will surely supply the intervention of all manner of persons to help out.

4. Speaking to energy with respect, passion and with uplifting ideas draws in more resources.

5. Fear is often more easily dispersed by changing one's purpose than by overcoming restrictions or *fixing* an attitude.

6. Be humble. Know that there are more people around you who have also had inklings of contact with spirit or who are also hungry for growth, or who are tired of the same things that tire you. Give them and yourself more credit in the fact that you are all connected. The person in the next office or at the next meeting may be ripe for a word—*a feel*—of encouragement. They are waiting to receive what they have been privately asking for.

7. Bring joy into an office, a hospital, a taxi, a school, a grocery store. Bring it because it could be used, and to overstep in this is far less of a concern than not daring to do it at all.

22. An Afterthunk

Picture the scene for this one. It was a hospital room. I was visiting a friend of ours. He'd been battling diabetes and other conditions. Things had become so serious that he'd had more than one close call with his life. Sitting with us was his wife, who had journeyed alongside him for months of illness. Along the way, she had picked up more than a little training about intention, healing, and healing techniques.

She approached his bedside, and began to move the palm of her hand in front of his chest in a circular motion.

"I'm picking up a lot of fear," she said as she approached him and gestured, moving her hand within a metre of his chest. "There are things that have to come out, that he has to let go of."

I sat and watched.

She continued, "I think there are past-life issues that have to be resolved. There's a lot of struggle . . ." And her diagnosis kept going as it identified negatives, blockages, and the like.

I'm polite, but I'm known to be firm. Knowing these two as I do, I was permitted a bit of slack.

"For heaven's sake, lady!" I butted in. "If you had tubes coming out of you and were in a hospital bed and had just had two close calls and couldn't walk away from someone listing off fears and blockages and issues and additional fights and struggles, what would happen to *your* energy!"

"It would shrink."

"And?"

"It would become fearful—"

"And? It would have more trouble healing. And it would get distracted. And it would be exhausted thinking there was that much more work to do and it would be natural that there would be some fear about the near-death experience he'd had and—"

I stopped myself short.

"Now, let's have a look at this. I'm very pleased you can feel and see and pick up what energy is doing. That is a key and a very important tool. Humour me for a second and watch this."

I had her repeat after me:

Ladies and gentlemen,

On behalf of all families strained by an illness among them, and on behalf of all spouses walking alongside an ill partner, and on behalf of all hospital patients lingering in bed in an atmosphere such as this, and on behalf of all persons with this man's combination of challenges, I'm going to show you what happens to a body when it is relieved of stress. I'm going to show you what happens when the partner is relieved of stress, and I am going to show you what happens to a person's healing abilities when they are relieved of stress. Watch this."

I asked her to gesture toward her husband again, in the same way she had done initially.

She said she felt "negative energy" leave him, his chest relax, his aura expand. And she reported a feeling of relief for herself. I also drew her attention to the energy in the room and what had happened as a result. Her feedback was of a similar uplifting nature.

In the end, the dedication of this woman contributed to a coming together of people and energies to pull her husband out of the danger zone. Her determination stayed, and her approach lightened up.

There was an unexpected and welcome result in addition to the help her husband received. She reported to me how, in confidence, doctors and nurses began to express how amazed they were at her husband's rebound from what had literally been death's door. And they invited her to consider actually showing them what she was up to. No wallflower, this woman had made no excuses about her work with energy and had unabashedly conducted it and taken a strong stance in being kept in the know about her husband's treatment as a person in her own right and on behalf of the rights of patients. Once again, a *"Who woulda thunk!"* had manifested itself in another corner of life.

It is momentum, one case at a time and one interaction at a time, which brings change. We look back on hideous social practices that we now see as damaging, ignorant, and of no worldly good, such as slavery and wholesale condemnation of races or groups. Correcting these behaviours is important. But just as significant is how we wield corrective force: with inspiration and compassion, and not in the belief that fighting will bring peace.

What had happened? In the first instance, the woman had attempted to extract something that she felt was negative and that she didn't want. This meant naming it, giving it energy and bringing it into the consciousness of the person(s) involved. In the second instance, she had—with some prompting—delivered *exactly* what it was she had felt was missing. She had delivered the goods, so to speak. And the environment instantly felt the difference and responded.

Some Thoughts:

1. *Become the healer you'd like to meet.* If you don't work consciously with energy, then you don't. But if you decide to do so, then for heaven's sake, make your own decision to do so with fun, ease and joy. Constantly naming negative energies and emotions only gives them power. *Trying* only brings on trying. Raising the notion of work and more work only brings on the strain of effort that in turn strains the body.

2. When aiming at any level to set an example, do so by all means and do so in ways that free us up. It is still not common knowledge or even a common sense of appreciation how energy and thought vibrate and function. Until the day comes when it is widely appreciated how our thoughts and energies affect one another, many people will grope for understanding and believe themselves to be incapable of influencing the atmosphere around them. As long as the process is still being played out, choose to be a person who brings **common sense** and **common decency** to your work.

3. Take time to think of yourself in the shoes of the client. What uplifts you may well go a long way to uplift them. We are not all that different from one another, and we are not all that separated, either.

23. The Art of the Spiritual High-Five

My first publisher, Dianne Thomas, who was instrumental in getting *The Thunder Within* on the bookshelves, had a passion about connecting people she believed had things in common or could help each other. One occasion when she pursued this with me, the three of us had the chance to demonstrate what healing does accomplish when it takes place at a higher vibration, for a higher purpose.

Dianne arranged a three-way call with a healer she had met in England and with whom she had continued to communicate by phone and mail as a source of guidance, inspiration and spiritual camaraderie. Since he happened to be on the road and was in Montreal, and we could not at the time go to see him, the second-best thing to do was to call him up.

As Dianne listened, this gentleman and I conversed, both fully aware of how much she had spoken to each of us about the other.

I took a chance.

"May I do something for you?"

"Why certainly!" came his response.

"Just a second. If you'd sit still, I am seeing something to the left inside your body next to your spine. Hold on a second while I work."

Using my visualization, I proceeded. The work was over in about fifteen seconds.

"Wow!" he exclaimed. How'd you *do* that?"

"What'd you get?"

"You just caused a deep boyhood fear I've been working on for years to simply vanish! I can feel such a shift, such a relief! Tell me how you did that!"

I explained to him that my work had nothing to do with content. That meant that I did not look for anything, had not perceived anything, had not been told by any sense or spirit to do anything, had not identified anything and did not care a hoot about the energy's origins, size, depth or connections. I had, as I believe is far more intelligent and useful, decided to do a bit of demonstrating. The recipe goes like this:

1. **Take** two healers/teachers. Choose those who are doing fascinating work and, in what makes obvious sense, are

functioning at different places on the globe so that revelations and joy spread more rapidly where they walk.
2. **Carefully remove** posturing, checking out, positioning, and poking.
3. **Add** respect, humour, fascination.
4. **Fold in** thankfulness for the work of each other.
5. **Whip up** the idea that it's about time the universe actually experienced how healers can meet in a way that teaches other healers to meet, other seekers to meet, other teachers to meet.
6. **Mix** gently with the declaration, "If I help this other chap out, his work will be more fun, more easy, more effective, more joyful and more expansive. He deserves to be helped out with a spiritual high-five. Show me what to do!"
7. **Bake** in a wide atmosphere that appreciates that all is watched and all is seen.

You will be left with a creation that is pleasant to the body, mind and spirit, spreads the word of fun, ease, and joy, and gets us past the notion that we need to work hard on ourselves. We parted ways both happier men. He for the relief, and me for the opportunity he gave to show what enhancing healing can do.

People can see. People can sense. Having recognized that truth, we spend much of our time teaching others or trying to get ourselves to refrain from noticing, mentioning, or bringing up other people's shortcomings, faults, dark sides, and the like. We end up splitting ourselves between the truth that we "see" and what to do with it.

Operating from a place where we are in forgiveness of others for what they may have built, and in empathy over what it might be like to live with any particular real or perceived restriction, what we see ends up to be a source of fascination, acceptance, and curiosity.

If you think you are working with blockages, issues, and such like, or matters you have not been able to take care of or look at or deal with or throw away, you have lowered the vibration of your intent, your work and your intervention. Hence the widely taught and wisely shared view that permission is needed if one is to "work" on another person.

On the other hand, if you put out the intention that along your path has come a man who is helping the world, and you wish to give him thanks and give him a gift for what he has done and is doing for others, you are not invading or checking or poking or sizing up. You are serving and giving gratitude that as a result of this encounter he will do even better work. You are not a healer in such an instance, you are a teacher. You are aware that the whole cosmos is watching and, as such, you have a great lot of students ready to get the point, thus saving themselves and others years of struggle or work or suffering.

We have become so accepting of what we have built as humans, that no other information is needed. It might be intellectually stimulating to find out why the fear got there, what caused it to be stored, how it was affecting him, and so on, but this is old-fashioned attention of the sort that often leads to psychobabble. Here, something refreshing has been created. *It's the art of the spiritual high-five.*

24. The Pub

I watched the toddlers strung along the length of a rope each was holding onto as they made their way across our path. We were wandering through a small Irish village. I had just gestured toward the community centre where this gaggle of children had gathered.

"Daycare," I observed to my wife Kathy.

"*Child minding!*" corrected a woman herding the youngsters into place as we passed, not bothering to look up at me at all, as if I should have had the sense to know the distinction. I half expected to have my face wiped, my mittens adjusted and to be admonished that obviously I had not slept as I should have at naptime. After all, we were in the land where two-lane highways are known as "dual carriageways," with nary a carriage in sight.

I should know. I'd just had a harrowing experience on a winding *single*-carriageway up the road. This was along a road with *no* shoulder 'tween a three-metre-high hedge to my left and an eighteen-wheeler crossing the line to my right and coming at me as if the local driver knew just by instinct that *of course* he would make it . . .

Child minding indeed.

It's not the children who mind in life. It's the adults. And it's the adults who secretly want to return to their knowingness as children. But if no one else around them is doing so, who's going to dare to be the first kid on the block to dare to be a kid again? We anecdote the *wise* things children say and the *silly* things adults say far more often than we do it the other way 'round.

Kath and I moved on. We eventually settled ourselves in a pub. There we struck up a conversation with the local Guinness deliveryman. Just by watching him we learned that true happiness—as this twenty-something expert showed us—is opening your toolbox with the air of a surgeon, laying out your instruments, and fine-tuning the handles and spigots in one of the seventy-five pubs you service in the county as if it were the only thing you wanted to do in all the world. (Except perhaps to get to Vancouver, which he had also done.)

We'd heard that the publican in *this* establishment doubled as the local undertaker, perhaps an Irish way to ensure that each of the departed gets at least a chance at a last one. Darned if this same gentleman—approaching eighty as he was and who'd left the region only once in his lifetime to try out a soccer match in England—wanted to know from us just what the latest news was in Quebec separatist politics and how the Montreal Canadiens were doing as a team. The Guinness never tasted so good. He was amazed at my knowledge of local history.

"I told him all he knows before ye got here!" corrected a local who had befriended us, looking for all the world like the prizewinner chosen for an international ad by the Irish Tourist Board.

There are many reasons why the genteel camaraderie and respect we found in that pub stays in my system. The energy it engendered was so welcome in those complicated times. To be sure, we discussed the

September 11th disaster—a date that may never again need be qualified by a year when mentioned in conversation—which had happened only three weeks before. While it certainly drew us together, it's a pity that such an event was succeeding in doing what we feel never can happen naturally or without effort.

The Ice Storm—crystallized in the minds of the people of central Canada as a pivotal event that shook the foundations of society in early 1997—sprouted anecdotes about endurance, spontaneous help and new lines of communication across communities. Then there are the tornados and the fires and the floods that get people talking to neighbours they normally never connect with. Disaster draws us to do it.

Yet, it seems, there are few people in the herd mentality of our society who have the inner strength to spark a sense of community that simultaneously crosses gender, ethnic, religious and class lines as a way of living. Few, that is, who seem to be able *to do so in times of tranquillity and peace.* What makes this so?

We remain blocked to the reality that we are at work in the service of our human gene pool. A joyous funeral sets the stage that ours will be joyous. A spontaneous letter giving thanks or congratulating someone would really be a child-like gesture. Come to think of it, what a surprise a handwritten, postal-delivered letter would be in itself!

Part of the wave of emotion that swept North America after September 11th was, in my experience, rarely mentioned. It was the unspoken shock so many people had about the feeling of being together—something in an active community-wide form that isn't part of the tribal vibration. It's the phenomenon that led a Toronto-area journalist to tell his viewers about a woman who'd been driving on the Don Valley Parkway (one helluva highway to those who know "T-O"). She had expressed how amazed she was at the conduct of the drivers in the days immediately following the tragedy, and that it had actually been possible for her to change lanes easily when she needed to!

Speaking of traffic, courtesy creates jobs. It helps to ensure customer traffic. Courtesy lowers health costs and absentee rates. Courtesy evokes and encourages neighbourhood discussion and safety programs. Courtesy helps to ensure that the innocence we so appreciate in children will become the unembittered joy of adulthood.

The next time you get together with a gang—be it driving a long distance with buddies or gathered 'round for a beer—tell the others of a favourite encounter you've had. It may have occurred yesterday, or it may have taken place years ago. And choose one for its spontaneity, its humour, its uplifting originality; and because it left you or someone else declaring, "You made my day!"

Somewhere in the offices of Canada's National Archives there's a message machine with my voice on it. It was a call I made to a staff member there to thank him for his help in finding me material for one of my books. He returned the favour, leaving me a message on *my* machine quite a while later. He'd called to say he was sorry that personal obligations had made an earlier reply impossible. He wanted to convey to me the message that it was so rare for a client to actually take the time to call back and express thanks that he'd decided to store my message on his machine. For months, he had been playing it on his "bad days" as a pick-me-up that, he reported, really worked.

When we know that we know that we make a difference, then we can choose how those differences are made. And we can learn to plant them and savour them and show others by demonstration and the presence of our energy how they're made and what comes of them.

A Thought:

We are "on" all the time, in that every single moment sends out its signal, be it one of confusion, joy, relaxation, fear or tension. That being the case, remember this truth and keep it in mind: As long as we *are* broadcasting, *bring* a sense of inclusion and relaxation to where you are, *bring* laughter and communication, peace and appreciation. You will find yourself in it when you bring it far more quickly than when you are looking for it.

25. Gotcha!

There was bound to be *one* exercise for you to do among these stories. And here it comes. The story entitled "Stop Stopping Doing This!" shed light on how much time people spend trying to overcome, let go, or get over. It need not be so difficult.

One of the easiest ways we have in making things harder—or one of the easiest means we have to make things easier—can be found in our use of language.

Let's take language as a topic for a moment, and look at how easy it can be to apply this important tool to making life easier. In other words, how do we stop stopping using language inappropriately?

Face it. Our tribe taught us how to use language, and some very significant people in our lives had a close hand in it. Few of us, however, have had a formal chance to stop and take a look at, or get a feel for, what language does to us and to others. Working at it becomes drudgery. Study it and you will begin to have fun.

I think that working on the self can be a bit of a drag. So why not look outside for a moment. Let's you and I take a look at two *other* people—more of a neutral territory—and observe what happens to *them*, depending on how language is being used. Here goes . . .

Think of two people standing in front of you. They are any two people, just representing two persons of no particular description. Have them face each other. They're now your partners in helping you decide and feel what sorts of declarations uplift yourself and others.

We can begin with some age-old favourites.

Have one person say to the other, *"You're going to have to change."*

Now look at the energy or feel the feeling around the speaker, then around the listener, then around the two of them. Consider the following:

- What happens to the energy in and around the person who is doing the speaking?
- What happens to how they both feel?
- How do you feel as a witness?

- What happens to the energy of the person who was the intended recipient of the statement?
- What happens to the energy around the two of these people as a single unit?
- What makes these feelings universal?
- What do you feel, being in their presence when this is going on?
- Does such a statement help to achieve what the speaker would like as an outcome?
- Does it motivate the intended recipient?
- Does it pull in enabling energy?
- What does it do to the surrounding energy?

You're learning *in the moment* about the physics of energy. It was ever thus. The physics of vibration and communication, the waves that are feelings, and the spirituality that is life are all intertwined. Go ahead and give yourself and others an *understanding* of energy and a comfort in studying it. As you embrace this means to empowerment, it changes the world as a whole.

Looking again at these two people, have one of them say the following phrases one at a time. After each declaration, stop and check the effect on the speaker, the effect on the listener or intended recipient, the effect on the energy around them, and the effect on you as a witness.

Try these out:

- I've never done this before.
- You are obviously afraid.
- Who do you think you are?
- I'm not very good at this . . .
- What do I do now?
- I'm picking up that you're uncomfortable.
- I'm probably going to screw this up.
- Don't you know how to learn anything?

- When are you going to get it?
- What's your problem?
- Can't you do anything right?

Especially notice the effects on the speaker when these phrases are said. Sometimes we're aware of what happens to the energy of the recipient, but not too many of us are aware that what we say to others has an effect on us as well.

On and on it goes. It's all vibrational, it's all electromagnetic, and it all has an impact.

If you could see it, what would it look like? Well, think of our society's widespread use of cellular phones. Each phone is sending out or picking up a signal that is travelling through the air at a particular vibration. And these are bouncing off relay towers that connect the phone to the landline telecommunications system. Think of all these people on cell phones crammed into a bustling downtown area of a big city. Now connect each of these phones with a laser beam of light. Spaghetti city! And we're walking through it all the time!

Mmmm. It bounces, vibrates and interferes. Did you know that, in October 2001, the Society for Psychical Research in London announced its belief that the increase in cellular phones was contributing to a dramatic drop in the sighting of ghosts and in the number of people contacting the group for aid in hauntings and sightings? Time to switch channels. But that's another chapter . . .

Language and the criss-crossed lines it creates behave no differently.

How could we bring an improvement to personal interaction that uplifts ourselves and others? To begin with, this is a perfect opportunity to embrace and use something else this book has looked at—the significance of bringing change on behalf of other people, also discussed in the story "Stop Stopping Doing This." We achieve this by practising universal principles of what it means to uplift energy.

1. Make a declaration about why you wish to improve your use of language. (See the story entitled "Listen Up!")
2. Celebrate the fact that, by using the "two people speaking" visualization, you now have a new tool in your toolbox to

check out your use of language. Give thanks that you're learning, not struggling.

3. Appreciate that you are becoming *fascinated* with how things work. That sure beats trying to fix something or trying *not* to do certain things.

4. Give voice to your appreciation and awareness that you are bringing old and wise yet new and refreshing means to grow and create unity and relieve stress.

5. Give thanks for the wisdom, of you and around you, that is helping you make this change.

6. Notice how much more energy you have and how much more calm you have around you when you are engaged in this.

7. Begin to notice how the use of language begins to improve, not because you have struggled at it or told yourself that you are going to have to stop old habits, but because you have literally and vibrationally become more attractive. It's simply more fun to be around you. And energy feels this! That's because people are energy; and energy is through, of and around people.

Sometimes people ask me, "How do I stop (there it is again!) from being affected by the language used by other people around me or against or upon me?"

Simple. Become fascinated with how they use language.

Turn once again to that visual of two people speaking to one another.

Now, what is the energy like that comes off a person who is *fascinated* about how people speak and how they learned to speak and why they speak the way they do? It's quite a bit different than someone worried and bothered and affected. How is the change achieved?

1. Love the person for how they were taught.

2. Know that your vibration alone is changing a room or a situation.

3. Know that your discretion and pure observation is teaching energy how it can behave.
4. Internally, thank the person for reminding you how energy functions; and reminding you about what works.

Let's close with a declaration. Speak this one out loud.

Ladies and gentlemen:

I would like you to notice what happens now that I have relaxed my use of language and have begun to appreciate my impact on my own life and the lives of others. Notice how much more relaxed I am becoming and how much more room there is in my body for oxygen and flow. And notice how my influence is expanding as I understand that everything vibrates. This means that my conduct is inspiring and sending out a message of how things can be done with fun, ease and joy. The media may never know of this, my neighbours may never know of this, but the cosmos knows. And that is what counts. Take a look at the energy around me, and notice the changes. Go and tell others. Thank you.

You are now in business, in active participation, building your reputation as to how you choose to learn and how you choose to set an example. Congrats!

26. You Go First!

Some years ago, James Burke hosted a BBC-produced series entitled *Connections*. He took viewers on winding paths through history, exploring the accidents, mistakes and the weave created by desires, necessity and circumstance that gave us certain of the traditions, practices, gadgets and concepts we have today. Would that each school system spent some time looking into this, giving youngsters an appreciation of how it is we have come to think.

In far too many places on the globe, the idea of simple practices and dialogue that make sense and would bring peace are just not done. Even the idea of religious leaders of two separate traditions sitting down for afternoon tea seems impossible in some quarters.

Breaking the ice, breaking the mould, breaking the boxes we live in can seem exhilarating and fun, fantastic and liberating, and also very, very scary. Like Christopher Columbus, or the Vikings setting out for the New World, *someone* has to be first. In our world, the biggest step does not have to be getting to the moon; it can be a Jew daring to say "good morning" to a passing Palestinian on a side street in Jerusalem.

Simple. Loving. Inclusive. And very, very scary.

All over the world, in the nooks and crannies of life, live people secretly working out something in their lives, be it the legacy of an alcoholic father, the memories of being sexually abused by someone in real or perceived authority, the fallout of being shunned by peers who are youngsters in the schoolyard, and the like.

And very few of these people attempting recovery or release or relief are having fun doing it. You'd think with so much of this type of angst going on, someone would come up with an easy, quick, effective and light-hearted form of blossoming beyond all the heaviness.

Mmmmmm. "Blossoming beyond."

Sure beats "moving on," doesn't it.

Why does it feel better?

Plants blossom. They don't rip out their roots. They don't declare, "I'm not going to get going until I let go!" They incorporate all that they are and integrate all that they are.

Wherever you are, whoever you are, you are the first person on the block to do *something*, even if it is to be the only citizen in the neighbourhood to have been a high school beauty queen and a year behind in filing your taxes and loving flower arranging and battling a fear of flying and not having visited Brisbane, Australia.

So it is with healing.

Take a look, for example, at the depth of bereavement some people experience around the passing of a favourite animal companion—a dog . . . a cat . . . perhaps a horse. At times the grief seems to surpass even what they think they'd feel in the case of the death of a person they know, even those who have been very close.

Here's a chance for such a pet owner to make a healthy declaration in their circumstance that they can and will demonstrate on behalf of all persons with pets, especially those who have garnered so much from their companions, how the passing of such a spirit can open up greater avenues. This can mean greater understanding of death, greater appreciation of the companionship we have, greater expansion of our knowingness about animals and something of a sense of what the animal itself feels, too! Here is a chance to embrace the energy that has built up between yourself and your pet and to use it to help yourself and others. Not only is it about a bereavement process, it's also about moving beyond that, even as you learn more about what makes such memories and connections so strong! You become a pioneer as much as a person giving yourself credit for what you are going through.

You hold your feelings in the palm of your hand, accepting that they are there, accepting what they are, and accepting that under the circumstances they make sense. These feelings are no longer something to get over or get rid of, but to embrace as a truth around you that can be transformed into an example.

In this way, a process that otherwise could have taken a long time, perhaps too long if a person were to take a look at her full life, takes on the characteristic of an inspiration. The original relationship then continues to have meaning—not only for the self, but for others.

It is up to someone to be first. Sometimes it will fall to a practitioner and therapist, and sometimes it will fall to the person who, in real or perceived terms, is going through a transformation.

I believe, perhaps in a rather radical way, that the idea of bereavement, as it is often manifested, becomes more of a struggle and a chance at self-judgment and recrimination than something that is refreshing, uplifting and freeing. The idea that only after we grieve are we free can instead become a matter of living in the moment in a way that says, "I have so much to do that my life is bigger and beyond this," or "My link with animals even in this role and way can help all humans and all animals."

Dare to bring joy to the life of another in a spontaneous way, like the couple I know who, without plans one New Year's Eve, decided to go door to door in their condominium and see in the New Year with neighbours they spontaneously invited over. Widows and widowers otherwise alone found themselves in a larger group in an unplanned but welcomed event that probably made the New Year's celebration *very new* indeed.

But **somebody** has to be first!

E.
Some Thoughts On What the Soul Already Knows

The amazing weave of experiences we produce as humans is reflected in the stories in this book. Each is based in part on universal principles of how energy functions. This is the fact that puts us on the crossroads where spirituality and religion, thought and action, belief and faith all meet. To be sure, the tragedy that struck New York and Washington on September 11, 2001, was deep, and it forever stamped its influence on the phrase "nine-eleven." However real the losses, the event, I believe, *did* reduce society to the bare bones of what matters. I call it *The World Trade Centre test.* Consider this:

If you ran up to the rubble of the World Trade Centre, and happened to see someone with arm outstretched from beneath the debris, would you not instinctively reach out and help pull that person from a potential grave without thinking of his or her gender, social status, income, or religion? At the same time, if you were that person in need of help would you not completely forget the significance of the age, race, gender, creed or social status of the person lifting you out?

Pity that we must get things down to such a level before we let go of all the things we work at that we would, in a flash, give up forever as unimportant.

Part of us seeks and part of who we are acts out. Within these ways of seeing the world there are many interpretations and boxes. Is it what is done to us, or is it what we do to others?

I have been asked, considering what I do, if I believe in God. Sometimes if I am in a certain mood, I might answer, "What's significant is the fact that the Old Fella, after all this time, still believes in *us*!" But yes, I certainly do.

"Is this a man of God?" A woman attending one of my talks confessed afterward that she had been prompted to ask this question under her breath as I was speaking.

"YES!" she reported had been the unequivocal answer that had come back. Reputation does travel. It is not that I believe that I am, it is what the universe reports to be true. If it were not true, I could try to fool you, but you cannot fool the cosmos. And especially not when you are beginning to trust yourself.

What religion can do to us by happenstance and interpretation was well illustrated to me by a man who conveyed how deeply he had been affected by a single incident long, long ago and had not been able to shake its adverse effects.

Well into his fifties, this gentleman would still break into tears telling of an incident that occurred when he was all of three or four years old. His mother, having entered the Catholic Church as a result of getting married, was not all that well versed in the High Holy Days of the Catholic calendar. It seems that on one particular day, she dropped her son and young daughter off at the preschool centre unaware that the nuns would be engaged in a day of prayer. The kids were left alone in the playroom where, in no time, each became engrossed in their own play.

Going with the flow of his spirit, this young boy began running around the room, and at one point went over to the pile of scrap paper in the room, gleefully flinging a handful in the air, scattering the pieces.

In a flash he noticed the towering figure of a black-clad nun over him. She held him by the scruff of the neck and with a stern voice admonished him, saying, "What a bad boy you are! Not even the Virgin Mary herself can love a boy like you!"

Well, in a split second, a message deeper than deep registered within this boy-to-be-a-man. And he struggled with it for decades to come.

All it took was a millisecond of a shift in the computer that we are. You'd think we'd know better by now.

These stories, involving teachers, peers, parents, television preachers and group leaders, are rampant. We resonate to the tale because so many of us have been there. Religion prompted the condemnation and, because religion was being taught as a thing of power and punishment involving sinners rather than as a spiritual expression of love and appreciation, the teaching and the admonition combined for a devastating effect. These effects are not logical; they run on belief and emotion.

What I have found to be accurate time and time again is that two things are going on. At one level is the boy's desire to fit into tribal beliefs (i.e. nuns are powerful, the Virgin Mary is super-powerful, and if *she* withdraws her love, man, are *you* in trouble cosmically!).

At another level, the boy's soul *knows* the woman is mistaken. (I'm referring to the nun here . . . You didn't actually *think* I was talking about *Mary*, did you?) Deep inside, the boy knows that:

- Nuns can't withhold someone else's love.
- Mary is her own woman and makes her own decisions.
- If we loved only good boys they would be trying to bargain for it.
- If we withheld it from bad boys they'd go looking for it elsewhere and in other ways.

When in a bargaining mode between what they *know* and what they *need* to position for, kids very often don't have the wherewithal for "Witty Retorts and Quick Comebacks" (a manual we should all be given at birth). We actually *know* that the nun's approach was not appropriate. It certainly had an effect, but it did not cause either the boy or herself to blossom. It may be argued that she was trying to do something positive; but she used a negative to do it. Thereby hangs a tale of how energy functions universally.

Once the boy-now-a-man was able to see this, he stopped trying to recover from the episode and instead embraced that which we all know works in the delicate balance of walking with our tribe and walking with wisdom. He ended up telling me of a time when, in the role as a client in the presence of a spiritual healer, he felt the Virgin Mary actually with him. Now he was able to put the two experiences together.

Our conversation moved on. One thing led to another and we found ourselves discussing how some people handle the subject of sex.

"Oh!" he said with laughter after obviously remembering some anecdote on the subject. "I don't even want to go there!"

"Send the nun."

He guffawed at my suggestion, letting out a healing laughter. These two separate incidents in his life were instantly framed in new meaning.

Gone was the effort to forgive her and forget—he no longer had to work at any aspect of that memory.

For me, a similarity has emerged between this nun-based drama and certain cases I've been asked to help out with concerning sexual abuse.

The impact of such events on children can be devastating. We need look only at the case of the molestation of boys by a staff member at Toronto's Maple Leaf Gardens stadium that resulted in the suicide of the principal plaintiff who broke the case open many years after the incidents. Although some catharsis must have taken place in his revelation of the incidents and in the subsequent settlement case, the real matter of *how* the man was holding the entire episode inside himself was obviously not resolved.

One of the most tragic parts of child molestation or sexual abuse has nothing to do with the event. It has to do with the amount of energy and thought that is consumed by the memory, sometimes for very, very long periods of time. I have been known to ask survivors of such events if they would enjoy having their sexuality back and no longer feel robbed of it.

The answer so far is a universal "Yes."

We move to a place of having them feel that it is all theirs again. Their soul knows that the act against them is at some deep place an attempt to gain something from someone else inappropriately and is an act that does not respect their sovereignty. The "bigger" and the "smaller" are two souls nonetheless, and they both contain knowingness. Keeping the targeted individual on a treadmill of recovery, loss, anger, grief, fear, and self-loathing doesn't even get close to fun, ease and joy. Both boys—the one in the playroom and the fellow at Maple Leaf Gardens—had a chance to pioneer new ways of thinking. Left without external examples of how to do this, they were left to their own devices. Bucking long-held trends in one's tribe that have not worked—and not worked for a *long* time—can seem daunting when we think of it as a game of push-and-pull. When we move from forcing change to one that causes new perspectives to blossom, we have really made a shift for ourselves and society.

The soul knows what makes sense.

The soul knows what sharing and fun and uplifting energy can produce.

The soul knows that positive interaction can build homes for the poor, reduce the stress that leads to illness, bring out the best in people, inspire co-operation, and move people's hearts and minds from woundedness to blossoming.

Because so many people have not had the chance in their lives to be shown how to reach out and help others, they don't know that they don't know how to do it. Because so many people have not had the chance to acknowledge when they feel something is not appropriate and that they need not be wound up or tied in knots, they don't know that they don't know how to recognize it.

The soul knows how the ripping of native peoples away from their heritage and placing them in government schools where they are punished for speaking their native tongue does not work. The soul knows that the spiritual vortex of energy created by a community in prayer together for peace produces one type of energy, while a gathering of the religious in prayers of hatred against another people creates another energy. The soul knows the difference between spirituality as a way of life and religion as a form of interpretation. And it knows the difference between seeking peace and finding it. It knows that more people living in a true sense of community reduces the incidents of sickness. And it knows that it knows we are capable of great things. These manifestations come even faster when we treat others with more respect and take to heart the reality that we are all connected.

It is the soul from which comes the declaration, "Gee, that makes a lot of sense," when we realize how much time is wasted on positioning and the emphasis on differences and separation. It is the soul that knows that the world could use some leadership and demonstrations of kindness. And it is the soul that knows we are all seen and all heard and that we all have an influence each and every day. That being the case, it is the soul from which we can operate to set an example in our own backyards of what can be achieved when we dare to bring ourselves and others along in our mutual greatness.

The soul already knows:
- A person supported by nutrition, untroubled sleep, hope, respect and purpose functions much more efficiently than one who is without these things.

- Common sense is universal. It transcends hatred, positioning and division.
- People who do not love themselves are less likely to positively succeed in a life that often asks us to love our neighbour as ourselves.
- Focusing on what is wrong about us and others has never really succeeded.
- Demonstrating what happens when we become the people we would like to meet can take courage, and it can produce feelings that are not only powerful, but—at first—very unfamiliar.
- Living from our boxes of gender, race, and creed in relating to the other gender, the other society, the other point of view has all been done before in zillions of dramas both unique and familiar. Doing things in a new way—often without a road map—is exciting. This calls us to once again embrace our creativity.
- Bringing light into the darkness is more effective than chasing away the darkness.
- Being wise is not necessarily about being open or advanced; it is about being innocent and uncomplicated.
- Finding evidence of the power of love is comforting; bringing evidence of the power of love is fulfilling.
- Whether working with hauntings, past lives, workplace conditions, inner children, outer adults, religion, posturing, advancements or backsliding, when one functions from the basis of principles, one need not ever change one's presence or bother about what is seen or heard.
- Truly advanced souls don't give a hoot about being advanced. That fact, in part, is what makes them advanced.
- If age-old wisdom cannot be practised, all the New Age positioning in the world doesn't amount to a hill of beans.
- Telling a person what she thinks and asking a person what she thinks can produce responses a world apart. Bringing

assumptions to a healing encounter produces results a world apart from what happens when one brings inspiration, love, advancement and celebration to the same session.

- Avoiding sin is harder work than demonstrating love. The former is work that is based on fear. The latter is inspirational and attracts energy that can hardly wait to be put to work.
- When you help babies, you help all babies; when you stay with the ill and challenged, you help all the ill and challenged; when you bring inspiration to the birthing and passing of souls you bring the same to all souls; and at the same time you raise the chance that when you go through it again you will be met with the same quality of interaction.

F.
Daring to Live What the Soul Already Knows

Marlyn Moffitt worked doggedly to keep me at the keyboard, and turned out pages of proofing as fast as I could produce them. Eager to get these words out on the street, she began telling me about my next writings even as I was preparing this book for you.

Our body of experience in providing assistance to others continues to grow. More and more people are gravitating toward the chance to share in discussion groups that have a deep spiritual purpose. Not able myself to find the opportunity to openly share with people how energy functions, I decided to take the initiative and invited others to gather. My intention was to create a free-flowing venue where we could have a fun, light, yet responsible sharing of what works in people's lives and what doesn't.

Not that we were consciously going after healing or psychic abilities such as those demonstrated by the television medium John Edward in his links with the other side. Nonetheless we noticed how energy began to be attracted to the very notion of our gatherings. It was encouraging to see people from different walks of life and spiritual and religious backgrounds sharing in the same space and in ways that actually inspire. It has been refreshing to be in a setting where many of the principles described in this book get a chance to be used and honed.

The experiences shared in the groups are rich with the type of material you discovered in these pages. Participants in these groups now total some eighty people, although we have not *yet* manifested the experience of getting them all together in one room! You know who you are. And for sure, the cosmos now knows more than ever who you are. We all thank you.

This of course doesn't exclude the vast numbers of visitors who don't at the moment have bodies. Friends and relatives, drop-ins and the curious all combine to manifest the lessons and laughter that characterize what happens when we remember to play.

Keep in mind that around the world, grand healing, easy transformation and miraculous changes are being manifested by wonderful souls. Many choose to work in anonymity, knowing that, after all, they too are seen far and wide in the first place, and are *very* known indeed. And, in other cases, people just haven't been caught on CNN or by the media in any form. Just because you haven't heard, doesn't mean it's not going on. Until we grow up enough to repel shams as useless wastes of time and decide to embrace truth as a fun, easy and joyous alternative, we will be tripping over arguments and demands for proof about what is real and what is not.

Many occasional visitors who due to circumstance have not had the opportunity to return to our groups have commented on the power of the energy in the room, and the openness, friendship and peace that accompany it. These qualities are not conjured. They emerge from the deep desire to demonstrate to the world what makes sense, and how easy things can be. Once again, energy has followed intent.

The day will come when discernment will be wide and open, but it will be used as a means to share and to help along. We won't be seeking out or playing with the "dark side" of anyone, including ourselves, because we will know that the alternative—using our gifts to grow, blossom, create and discover—is far more uplifting, enlightening and enlivening. Go and demonstrate. As you do so (a most wise form of teaching), someone in your life may stop and exclaim, "Why didn't *I* think of that!"

Then you too will have tales to tell and adventures to share. What will happen?

My wife Kathy once asked me if men's suspenders fall off the shoulder the way a woman's bra straps do. It was an innocent enough question formed from reading a newspaper article on men's attire.

Thank goodness I was on the ball.

Had I said "Yes," I might have had some explaining to do indeed.

Had I said "No," I would have been in exactly the same position.

So, I simply said, "I don't know." Then I explained how a millisecond of wise contemplation had saved me endless trouble. And so, in answer to my final question that I posed to you, I will say, with great anticipation, readiness and curiosity:

"I don't know! But my soul already does."

About the Author

John Heney was born in Montreal in 1956 and lived in Toronto and Stratford, Ontario, before embarking on formal study and professional work in journalism, public policy and international affairs. Felled suddenly at the age of thirty-five by the effects of cerebral palsy and the mysterious and sudden onset of a movement disorder called dystonia, he set out to recover his functions.

While concentrating on the personal quest he chronicled in his book *The Thunder Within*, he found himself being called upon, more and more, to coach others, and in ways and circumstances he could not have imagined in his wildest dreams. From this has emerged his practice in—as one observer has called it—whatever it takes to cause a person to blossom and become the best they can be. It's what John calls *spiritual mechanics*.

His work has taken him to many audiences, including a national conference on wellness in the workplace sponsored by the Conference Board of Canada, and as a speaker at a groundbreaking conference on Spirituality in Health Care at the University of Toronto. Through his writing, coaching, teaching, and public speaking, he demonstrates the power that creativity and common sense can have in our lives when we take the time and apply the awareness to let them flower.

John and his wife Kathy live in Ottawa, Canada. They enjoy Scrabble™, travel, the practice of *qi gong* and the companionship of the many friends they are gifted to know. Far from calling what he does in the kitchen mere "cooking," John "creates with love" over a stove, often to the tune of a 1920s fox trot as he indulges in his passion for antique gramophones and the early days of the recording industry.

To order more copies of John Heney's books:

For
Ladies and Gentlemen!
Daring to Live What the Soul Already Knows

In Canada send $19.95 plus $6.00
Elsewhere send $17.95 US plus $6.00

For
The Thunder Within

In Canada send $24.95 plus $6.00
Elsewhere send $19.95 US plus $6.00
(Surcharges cover GST, shipping and handling)

Send your orders to:

GENERAL STORE PUBLISHING HOUSE
Box 28, 1694B Burnstown Road
Burnstown, Ontario, Canada K0J 1G0
Telephone 1-800-465-6072
Facsimile (613) 432-7184

You can order on-line at:
http://www.gsph.com

VISA and MASTERCARD accepted

John Heney can be reached at: jjheney@netrover.com